STRATEGICALLY
TRANSFORMING
THE
Mortgage
Banking Industry

D1416039

ALSO BY JAMES DEITCH

Hacked. Screwed. Gone.:
An A-Z Blueprint to Protect Your
Business from Accidental & Malicious
Information Security Threats

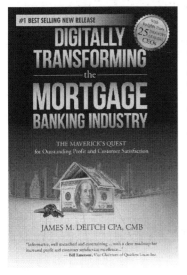

**Digitally Transforming the
Mortgage Banking Industry:**
The Maverick's Quest for
Outstanding Profit and Customer
Satisfaction

STRATEGICALLY TRANSFORMING

THE

Mortgage

Banking Industry

*Thought Leadership on
Disruption from Maverick CEOs*

JAMES M. DEITCH CPA, CMB

DEDICATION

The MBA Opens Doors Foundation is a non-profit organization dedicated to aiding families with a critically ill or injured child by making their mortgage or rent payment. MBA Opens Doors currently works directly with nine childrens' hospital to identify families in need.

Opens Doors holds a special place in my heart. All royalties from this book will be donated to the Opens Doors Foundation.

ACKNOWLEDGEMENTS

Thank you to Judy, my wife, for encouragement, assistance, and practical advice, and most of all for being a role model and mother to our kids.

To my children Michael and Christina, and grandchildren Marie, Belle, Colin, and Caroline for your constant inspiration.

To Alex Henderson, my friend, business partner, and consigliere for thirty years, who more or less kept me out of foolish adventures and helped greatly in the concept, structure and story arc of this book.

To Don Bishop for 45 years of friendship, business, good wine, fun, and for being a successful fellow entrepreneur.

To Rob Peterson and Maylin Casanueva for your strategic knowledge and perspectives on mortgage banking and capital markets and for helping our business clients in so many ways.

To Dave Stevens, who has been a business inspiration to me since his time with FreddieMac. Dave was diagnosed with cancer in February 2017. Since then, Dave has lived his life as an outstanding example of personal courage, determination and selflessness in his ongoing fight with cancer. He provided his outstanding service to

MBA through his retirement in August 2018. Dave continues to influence the industry as a thought leader and advocate.

To the Mavericks: Barrett Burns, Bill Cosgrove, Bill Emerson, Brent Chandler, Brian Fitzpatrick, Cody Pearce, Dave Stevens, David Motley, Deb Still, Ed Robinson, Eddy Perez, Gene Lugat, Jerry Schiano, Jonathan Corr, Julie Piepho, Kevin Pearson, Marcia Davies, Martin Kerr, Matthew Durkee, Nathan Burch, Nima Ghamsari, Patrick Sinks, Patty Arvielo, Phil DeFronzo, Richard Bechtel, Rick Arvielo, Rose Marie David, Ross Diedrich, Stanley Middleman, Steve Schwalb, Susan Stewart, and Tim Nguyen. Thank you so very much for your willingness to share your thought leadership. Without your thought leadership, this book would not be possible.

To Mauricio Valverde for your assistance in interviewing the Mavericks, research, and your drafting help of the Information Security chapter.

To Eleni Valasis for your outstanding writing, editing, and research work. Thank you!

To Anthony Nguyen for technical research, analytics, and helping with the production of the manuscript. To Brett Hamsher and Pam Mennie for analytics and research assistance. To Barb Wise for all your design and graphic work over the years.

To Teraverde®'s collaborators, clients, and friends – you make this all possible!

FOREWORD
ALEX HENDERSON

Jim Deitch's first book on mortgage banking transformation, *Digitally Transforming the Mortgage Banking Industry*, — an instant best seller — was conceived by Jim at the 2017 MBA Chairman's Conference. The industry was experiencing higher costs to produce and profit was under pressure. The average earnings of Independent Mortgage Bankers were released the second day of the Conference – 11 basis points on loan production, well below the long-term average of about 50 basis points.

Jim served on a panel headed by Bill Emerson of Quicken which focused on the cost to produce and turnaround time. The idea at the Conference was that better deployment of technology would transform the mortgage banking business. Jim came up with a brilliant idea for a book — what if he interviewed highly successful transformative mortgage industry CEOs to find out what worked in the real world. Would they be willing to be quizzed on their secrets by someone who knew what questions to ask?

Digitally Transforming the Mortgage Banking Industry was born. Amazingly fifty CEOs agreed to be interviewed by Jim. Twenty-Five CEOs Jim found to be "Mavericks" willingly shared their thinking and secrets of success with Jim. As noted by a number of reviewers, the book contained "great insights from some of the best known names in the industry" with "an amazing roster of mortgage banking heavy hitters interviewed for their opinions on where the industry needs to go to stay productive and competitive."

Digitally Transforming was a best-seller – the #1 new release on Amazon in its category. Although several reviewers found that the book was "a remarkably compelling look" with "behind the scene insights from leaders within the industry" reviewers also stressed Jim's own "incisive thinking" in developing the book's themes. As one reviewer noted "None of the many Mavericks who've generously shared their thinking own the whole story; it took someone to put them together for a clear picture to emerge."

The year after the 2017 conference was very turbulent. The 2018 MBA Chairman's Conference focused on disruption of the industry by a variety of forces including low housing inventory, shifting consumer expectations, and another profit tremor announced at the conference: 60% of Independent Mortgage Bankers lost money and the average earnings of IMBs in the most recent reported quarter was a loss of 9 basis points on loan production.

Averages are deceiving and some IMBs and lenders are achieving excellent profit performance, but most are not. The reader of this book will hear from executives that deployed the approach described in *Digitally Transforming* and found considerable success. However, in this follow-up book Jim takes his incisive thinking and business acumen to a new level. The reasons for the widely varied performance are manifold, as discussed in this book. Those many reasons led to this follow-up book with a new title: *Strategically Transforming the Mortgage Banking Industry.*

Technology is of course a key lever of industry transformation, but the economic landscape has changed tremendously since the 2017

MBA Chairman's conference and requires mortgage bankers to consider additional strategic levers. Tight housing inventories, rapid home appreciation, rapid evolution of big data, changing consumer preferences and expectations, and a regulatory environment more cognizant of the damage from regulatory excess have emerged. The private label securities market and QM safe harbor for banks under $10 billion in assets will have major industry impact.

The tone at the 2018 Chairman's Conference was decidedly different than 2017. Transformation was still top of mind, but the focus had expanded: <u>Strategic</u> Transformation, not just <u>Technological</u> Transformation, which is why Jim decided to write a second book, *Strategically Transforming*. To address the timely nature of strategic transformation, Jim decided to release this book 120 days from the 2018 Chairman's Conference. That's a very fast timeline to conceive, research, and write a follow-up book. But speed to address this important issue is critical.

The need for speed is becoming a defining factor in the shape of our industry, as is clear from Jim's discussions with the Mavericks in this book. Many of the Mavericks interviewed in the first book are revisited for their strategic insight. New Mavericks have been identified.

The concept of the Maverick as a transformational element also led Jim to use technology to create the *MaverickCEO.com* website to provide continual access to thought leadership from the Mavericks and industry leaders. It is a worthwhile visit.

ABOUT THE AUTHOR

James M. Deitch founded Teraverde® seven years ago, after serving as President and CEO of five federally chartered banks over twenty-five years. Teraverde® now advises over 150 clients in mortgage banking, capital markets, and financial technology, ranging from some of the largest U.S. financial institutions to independent mortgage bankers to community banks. Jim founded two national banks, including a top 50 national mortgage lender.

Jim holds a Master of Business Administration, with concentrations in Finance and Marketing, and a Bachelor of Science degree in accounting from Lehigh University. He is a Certified Mortgage Banker and, until he realized mortgage banking was a lot more interesting than public accounting, practiced as a CPA. Jim has been a director of both publicly traded and privately-owned banks and lenders through some very interesting times.

Jim's experience in residential mortgage banking for the last three decades on a retail, wholesale, and correspondent basis led to an intense desire to learn about how technology and other strategic levers could be applied to financial institutions. His experience includes multi-channel loan origination and sales management, mortgage product design, credit policy, hedging, securitization and loan servicing, and his beginning to end experience – and his love of high-performance aircraft —has fueled his "need for speed" in applying strategic thinking to mortgage banking.

He has served on the Mortgage Bankers Association Residential Board of Governors and served as a CEO panelist and speaker for major financial institutions, financial industry associations, corporate clients, the Department of Defense, and universities. Jim is a thought leader and has published numerous articles in the industry publications, including the best-selling book, "Digitally Transforming the Mortgage Banking Industry," published in February 2018. Jim lives in Naples, Florida.

MAVERICK	TITLE	COMPANY
Barrett Burns	CEO & President	VantageScore Solutions, LLC
Bill Cosgrove	CEO	Union Home Mortgage
Bill Emerson	Vice-Chair	Rock Holding Inc.
Brent Chandler	CEO & Founder	FormFree Holding Corporation
Brian Fitzpatrick	CEO	LoanLogics, Inc.
Cody Pearce	President	Cascade Financial Services
Dave Stevens	CEO & President (retired)	Mortgage Bankers Association
David Motley	President Colonial Savings, F.A. and its divisions	Colonial National Mortgage
Deb Still	CEO & President	Pulte Mortgage, LLC
Ed Robinson	Senior Vice President, Head of Real Estate Lending	USAA
Eddy Perez	President	Equity Prime Mortgage, LLC
Gene Lugat	Executive Vice President of Strategic Support	PrimeLending, Inc.
Jerry Schiano	CEO	Spring EQ
Jonathan Corr	CEO & President	Ellie Mae, Inc.
Julie Piepho	President of National Operations	Cornerstone Home Lending, Inc.
Kevin Pearson	President	CalAtlantic Mortgage, Inc.
Marcia Davies	COO	Mortgage Bankers Association
Martin Kerr	President	Bestborn Business Solutions
Matthew Durkee	Executive Vice President & President of New England Markets	NBT Bancorp, Inc.
Nathan Burch	CEO & Principal	Vellum Mortgage, LLC
Nima Ghamsari	CEO & Co-Founder	Blend
Patrick Sinks	CEO	Mortgage Guaranty Investment Corporation
Patty Arvielo	President and CoFounder	New American Funding
Phil DeFronzo	CEO & Founder	Norcom Mortgage
Richard Bechtel	EVP, Head of US Mortgage Banking	TD Bank
Rick Arvielo	CEO	New American Funding
Rose Marie David	EVP Director of Mortgage Lending	HomeStreet Bank
Ross Diedrich	CEO & Founder	Covered Insurance
Stanley Middleman	CEO	Freedom Mortgage Corporation
Steven Schwalb	CEO & Managing Partner	Angel Oak Home Loans LLC
Susan Stewart	CEO & Founder	SWBC Mortgage Corporation
Tim Nguyen	CEO & Co-Founder	BeSmartee

Note: Titles are as of interview date

TABLE OF CONTENTS

CHAPTER 1

A CHANGING LANDSCAPE

"In mortgage banking, there is no strategy. The government tells you what to do. You do it or face litigation and enforcement. That's why the business is so commoditized." This is a startling assessment of the state of the mortgage banking business and comes from an executive in the industry. This individual was serious. Many in our industry appear to accept the 'no strategy' view of our business. If you concur, then read no further.

In my opinion, 'no strategy' cannot be the answer, especially at this point in mortgage banking's history.

I can understand why so many are entrenched in the idea of 'no strategy.' It's true that the residential housing and lending space in the United States is one of the most regulated areas of the economy— sometimes oppressively regulated. It may sometimes feel like regulators 'tell you what to do.' But there are many choices that can be freely made by mortgage executives. Some executives, in fact, are rapidly examining strategy and becoming disruptors in the mortgage banking business.

There *are* choices—strategic choices. We need to learn from these as an industry and learn to leverage these proactive solutions across mortgage banking. Our culture and industry are going through some seismic changes and it behooves us to keep up, adjust, and leverage true and active strategy against a 'shifting tide.'

In many ways, this book is about strategy and not specifically mortgage banking. It's about strategy applied to mortgage banking. Why the nuance? My first book, "Digitally Transforming the Mortgage Banking Industry," dealt with the application of digital transformation to the mortgage banking industry and process. The response to the book was very gratifying. The book became a best seller in its category and it generated thousands of dollars of royalties that were donated to the Mortgage Bankers Association Opens Doors Foundation.

Shortly after the book was published, a well-known CEO in the industry and I sat down for coffee. "Jim, do you know how to make a small fortune in mortgage banking?" I knew the punchline, but I let him deliver it. "Start with a big one." he quipped. And for good reason, as costs have escalated and profits have fallen in the mortgage banking industry.

David Motley, 2017 Chairman of the Mortgage Bankers Association and President of Colonial Savings, noted that he was "struck by how the government plays such a huge role in our mortgage finance process. The expansive regulatory structure put in place after the financial crisis of 2008 has really impacted consumers' ability to achieve homeownership. The impact of regulation can be seen in the increasing cost of originating a mortgage":

Cost per Loan

Source: MBA Mortgage Bankers
Performance Report

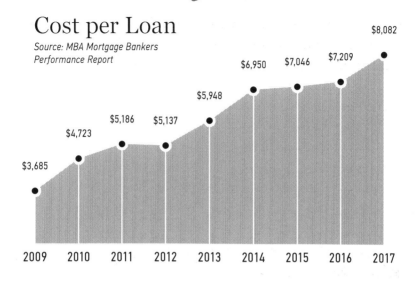

$8,082

$7,209

$7,046

$6,950

$5,948

$5,186 $5,137

$4,723

$3,685

2009   2010   2011   2012   2013   2014   2015   2016   2017

The cost increases include a roughly 50% increase in the number of non-sales personnel at a typical mortgage bank. In 2010, the personnel mix of a mortgage banker was approximately 60% in origination personnel and 40% in operations personnel. That mix has reversed. There are now 60% in operations and 40% in origination.

Said another way, in 2010, a company of 400 employees would have about 240 origination personnel and about 160 operations personnel. In 2017, a 400 employee company would have 240 in operations and 160 in origination.

Employee Mix

2010   vs   2017

Source: MBA Mortgage
Bankers Performance Report

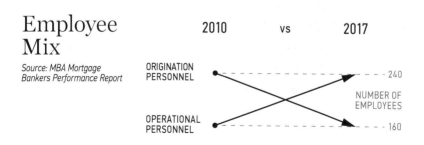

ORIGINATION
PERSONNEL

OPERATIONAL
PERSONNEL

240

NUMBER OF
EMPLOYEES

160

It's not just regulatory burdens that have increased costs. Sales and operations compensation costs eat up 60% of the revenue of a mortgage lending operation, shown below in basis points:

Compensation Compared to Total Revenue		
Source: MBA Mortgage Bankers Performance Report		31.2 - PROFIT
		118.5 - ALL OTHER COSTS
		18.9 - MANAGERIAL PERSONNEL
		28.2 - BENEFITS
TOTAL REVENUE 379.1	TOTAL COMPENSATION 229.4	79.7 - OPERATION COMPENSATION
NET REVENUE 39.5%	COMPENSATION TO REVENUE 60.5%	102.5 - SALES COMPENSATION

My coffee with the CEO continued as we discussed the cost and compensation structure of the industry. "Jim, this is just crazy." he continued. "Mortgage banking is the process where production people systematically loot shareholders and owners of all of their equity… they squeeze virtually every dollar out of a company and move on to the next sucker. They'll continue to do this until we have the stones to change the industry strategy."

I felt this CEO's pain. It's been a difficult year for many lenders. The CEO said, "A lot of us have the stones to change the business structure. I just don't want to be first to reduce compensation to originators." I understood. The first one through the door often gets roughed up pretty well.

JAMES M. DEITCH CPA, CMB

After the meeting, my mind wandered to a lunch discussion I had with Billy Beane, an executive with the Oakland Athletics, shortly after the movie "Moneyball" had premiered. Billy gave a presentation at the MBA's Chairman's Conference to a small group of CEOs. His talk recounted how he had to let highly paid, 'big name' players go because of compensation constraints for the team.

Beane spoke about finding undervalued baseball players who could work in a collaborative manner so that the A's could compete with teams that had "star" players. Billy's goal, in fact, was to develop a team that could compete and win against much better-financed opponents without any big name, big pay 'stars' at all.

I happened to sit next to Billy for lunch after his presentation and took the opportunity to probe more on the data-driven strategy that Billy had implemented at the Athletics. He described the strategy: "It's about winning games at the least cost. We're a small market team and can't afford to pay the salaries of large market teams. But we can still compete and win as long as the cost of winning a game fits our budget."

I said, "So you manage differently."

Billy laughed. "Our budget forced us to find a strategy that allowed us to manage differently and win." And Mr. Beane found that strategy and has continued to use it successfully. I thought again about my conversation with my distressed CEO friend. "Manage Differently" ... and win.

I spoke with Billy Beane again in early September 2018. We spoke about the A's use of a data driven strategy over time, and its relation to residential lending. And in identifying undervalued assets, whether they are baseball players, originators or investment securities. More on that later.

I also recently spoke with Dave Stevens, retired CEO of the Mortgage Bankers Association, about the industry. The discussion immediately moved towards overvalued assets, specifically some (but not all) loan officers. This book is not about loan officer compensation, but it's clear this is a topic with strategic consequences. Here are Dave's thoughts:

> "Mortgage lending is now a commodity business. There are a lot of reasons for that. Under Dodd-Frank, many product variations and features are effectively outlawed. We standardized disclosures across the board. And for most of America, the product choices are a homogenized 30-year fixed rate or 15-year fixed rate product. And sure, there's some adjustable rate lending and non-QM lending for 10 to 15 percent of the marketplace. But we pay mortgage loan officers 120, 150 basis points or more to sell a commodity mortgage product. Thirty-year fixed rate loans. $8,000 of cost per loan. And it makes no strategic sense. The industry overvalues many loan officers. It won't continue.
>
> The industry will be disrupted by competitors that differentiate product, help the consumer make sound choices for their circumstances, become customers for life, and do it by manufacturing defect-free loans quickly and efficiently.
>
> That's not the current model. Competitors that implement strategies that offer differentiated product, sound advice, build relationships, and generate clean loans efficiently are going to win."

Susan Stewart of SWBC weighed in on compensation versus value added:

"Most companies can afford to pay 100 basis points for origination, but companies are paying more than that. Without question that is setting companies up to give away all profits. This isn't sustainable.

It would be really great if some changes are made to compensation requirements. The industry needs some carve-outs for the loan officer to participate in a price concession and sharing in that. But you don't allow them to raise the price. This will correct the problem the industry has right now. And it is clearly really significant."

Eddy Perez of Equity Prime said:

"Dodd-Frank was the greatest LO pay increase in the history of mankind. What we have now is the loan officer not accountable for any errors or mistakes and they can demand 250 basis points for doing a poor job for the company and for the consumers. And that's just crazy.

The biggest misfortune is that regulators don't think about the impact on the end consumer. They don't realize the cost impact and that's where the real shame of it is."

Ed Robinson of USAA summed up the industry views on loan officer compensation:

"I was with a group of my peers and we all were of the mindset that LO comp has to change. Nobody wants to be a first mover or second mover. Everybody wants to be third in line for this. From a profitability standpoint, all you have to do is look at what happened with margins post Dodd-Frank. Clearly, an unintended consequence. Clearly an area that needs to be addressed.

Every single leader that I know of in the industry is struggling with this. LOs are highly compensated for the amount of work they do especially given the digital age. You're starting to see less and less work having to be done by the MLOs and you're starting to see a lot more of that being tailored to digital capabilities.

We have to find a way to right size the compensation. We've found ways to take some of the fixed cost component out of the value chain. [What's left] is regulatory compliance costs and LO compensation."

What Dave, Susan, Eddy and Ed are saying is that compensation regulations are part of the large issues our industry had that make it difficult, but not impossible to manage differently. While regulatory change is possible, we have to think about a strategy to 'Manage Differently.'

STRATEGY IN MORTGAGE LENDING

Strategy seems to be on a lot of CEOs' minds. Rick Bechtel of TD Bank offered a look at the innovative side of strategy:

"Unbelievably fascinating things are going on in terms of the way we will assemble data. Consumer direct particularly will change given big data. It's the predictive ability to go to consumers whether they're in your portfolio, whether they're in your bank, or whether they're just out there in the world.

The predictive ability to offer a financial solution before the consumer may even realize they need the solution is at hand. Much like Netflix knows what movie I should be watching tonight or Amazon knows what I should be buying next or that it's time to buy it.

This is the essence of predictive strategy and some lenders are applying this strategy now. Others will soon follow. This is truly a game-changing strategy."

Ed Robinson of USAA discussed some of the strategic challenges facing the industry:

"The key is knowing how and when to engage with customers in the manner they want. It's the one area that I've seen companies fall short on. And not just in this industry. You'll devise some new capability to engage consumers and then they get to a point where they have a question. Everything they're doing is on their phone or their iPad. And all of a sudden, you tell them you need to call such and such. And so you've completely ruined the experience for the consumer.

Especially when the target demographic is the millennial, who is much more tech savvy than we will ever be. There's an element of knowing who is your target customer, how does that customer want to engage, and then how do you enable that engagement in the manner that customer best sees fit?

You've got to make sure that you have transparency. That means transparency in process, transparency of offerings, and transparency of progress to not only the consumer but to the key stakeholders such as the realtors. You've got to have 'off ramps' so that as soon as there's a question or a concern that you have the channels built so the customer can get the information when they want, how they want.

It should not just be a point of sale contact nor should it be just an origination contact. It's got to be there over the entirety of the consumer life cycle. We have to make sure that the customer has a meaningful experience that not only attracts but keeps the customers."

Gene Lugat of PrimeLending noted borrower preferences are changing traditional retail strategy:

"Over 90 percent of borrowers choose text as their primary source of communication. That's an adaptation that we've made. And we also see that same consumer is much more likely to be able to provide or want to provide a singular verification component that we're using today to cut down on paperwork. Our strategy is to be more focused on delivering education and product information and to better educate the consumer and strengthening that relationship at the point of sale."

Rose Marie David of HomeStreet Bank added these thoughts on strategy:

"There's sort of two stages that drive strategy. The first is the transformational shift that is occurring because of the digital age. So, you have a need to transform your business to remain relevant. And then you have the second, with the cost construct in our business that came as a result of the Dodd-Frank compensation regulatory changes and the increasing cost of compliance. All of this bled over to the increasing cost of manufacturing a loan. So, we just have significantly increasing cost structure. Now we have that perfect storm of overcapacity leading to margin compression."

There is a relationship and empathy side of the business— this is undeniable. People don't get a mortgage just to get a mortgage; they use the mortgage to buy, afford, and enjoy a home *for their family.* That is something lost on the bureaucrats who think in sterile terms about "ability to repay" and "Appendix Q." We may think we have the best intentions, but the empathy has largely gone out of lending.

Eddy Perez covered this point well:

> *"I've sat in meetings where people suggest if you lend below a 620, you're a bad person. I'll be honest with you; our strategy lets us go down to 550 and those loans are 10 percent down with reasonable DTI ratios. So, you're not compromising the underwriting, because when you dig into the customer's story, it's about life events. It's divorce or something medical. We have the power to make loans that we believe will perform, and we are accountable for that."*

With so many C-level leaders talking about so many aspects of strategy, I undertook this book, "Strategically Transforming the Mortgage Banking Industry," as my contribution to the discussion.

STRATEGIC LEVERS

What are we talking about when we cite 'strategy?' One definition of strategy is, "a plan of action designed to achieve an overall aim."[1] This book defines strategy as the following:

---

[1] Google definition of strategy.

A plan of action to achieve three simultaneous goals: superior profitability, outstanding customer satisfaction, and defect-free loans.

What strategy is not: cutting margins, layoffs, adding volume for volume's sake etc. Those are tactical decisions, not strategy. The aim of strategy is to achieve the objectives of superior profitability, outstanding customer satisfaction, and defect-free loans. These three objectives can be achieved in a variety of ways through what I identify as strategic levers.

There are six broad strategic levers to achieve a lender's goals;

1. A lender can expand to achieve **economies of scale**. This strategy seems very common. Grow the volume that runs through an originator and 'all will be well'. Expansion for economies of scale can include hiring sales personnel, Loan Officers, Account Executives, and adding geography to serve. Economies of Scale strategy includes mergers and acquisitions. Economies of scale do not include outsourcing; outsourcing is a process transformative strategy lever.

2. A lender can adjust its **channels of distribution**. This includes adding channels such as direct-to-consumer, traditional retail, wholesale, correspondent, bulk purchase, and realtor or builder joint ventures.

3. A lender can become **technologically and process transformative.** This includes execution excellence, process automation, robotics, big data and additional technology for augmenting core applications such as LOS, etc.

4. A lender can exploit **product niche or niches.** Product niches can include non-QM, rehab, construction-to-perm, fix and

flip, investment property, alternate income qualification methods, etc.

5. A lender can **diversify** beyond consumer mortgage banking. This includes consumer lending, home equity lines of credit, insurance, commercial real estate lending, wealth management, etc.

6. A lender can increase the level of **relationship and empathy** when interacting with prospects, customers, and employees. It's forming a long-term relationship beyond a single mortgage transaction or series of transactions.

These levers can be expressed on a strategy map. We'll cover the map in more detail later on, but I want to introduce it now to help the reader visualize the strategic levers.

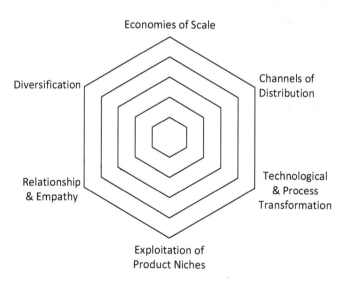

As mentioned, my first book, "Digitally Transforming the Mortgage Banking Industry," focused primarily on lever 3, Technological and Process Transformation. The book rapidly became a bestseller and I appreciate the hundreds of positive comments and suggestions regarding the book. I really appreciate, too, the stories from the many executives that applied the Digital Transformation process and achieved success in their respective businesses. Here's one story from a Chief Marketing Officer of a mortgage banker:

> *Our COO recently gifted me your book, "Digitally Transforming the Mortgage Industry," and it instantly changed the way I view our business and provided me with a fresh perspective on how to drive success through the lens of digital technology. The story about your daughter buying a car with ease in relation to the convoluted process of purchasing a home stuck with me. It is obviously one of the largest opportunities for the mortgage industry, next to decreasing the cost of production.*

But the issue of strategy has become much more acute in the past twelve months. Margins are compressed, refinance volume is substantially reduced, and disruption of the lending landscape is becoming more apparent.

THE LONG VIEW

A discussion of strategy necessarily must begin with the expansive and long view of the business, political, and economic landscape and identifying where opportunities and threats lie.

With regard to the political landscape, it's easy to allow the incivility that appears to be ever present in our country today to create a pessimistic outlook. The fact is, however, the United States has been the land of opportunity for over 200 years. The naysayers of today ignore perhaps *the* central characteristic of the U.S.— the draw that the land of opportunity offers. As Dave Stevens of MBA notes, many new household formations and homeowners will be immigrants as the makeup of the population continues to evolve. We have always been a nation where immigration played a substantial role in population growth.

The apocalyptic cries and pessimism of today remind me of the fears of four decades ago when former MIT professor Lester Thurow wrote "The Zero-Sum Society: Distribution and the Possibilities for Economic Change." He presented a lecture in Boston in the early 1980s that served as a laundry list of sobering predictions: the United States would run out of petroleum reserves by 2000, the northeast would be uninhabitable due to oppressive energy prices, Japanese manufacturing expertise would render the United States industrial base obsolete, and other doomsaying prognostications. None of Thurow's predictions came to be. The graph below shows U.S. household net worth increasing by a factor of ten since Dr. Thurow made his predictions. This illustrates that myopia can influence the worldview of even a well-educated economist[2].

---

[2] https://www.nytimes.com/2016/03/30/business/economy/lester-c-thurow-prominent-economist-is-dead-at-77.html

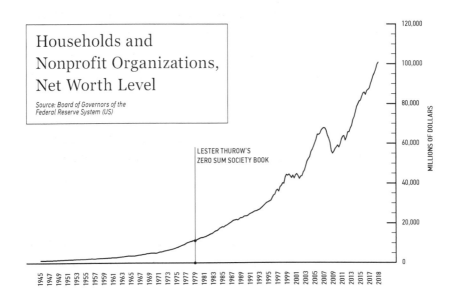

Households and
Nonprofit Organizations,
Net Worth Level

Source: Board of Governors of the
Federal Reserve System (US)

LESTER THUROW'S
ZERO SUM SOCIETY BOOK

MILLIONS OF DOLLARS

Readers should know my worldview for this book: the United States possesses and will maintain an unparalleled group of geographic, demographic, and historic advantages that even the most feckless of political leaders are unlikely to significantly disturb in our children's lifetimes. The republic has a great deal of resiliency and the United States is not a zero-sum society.

Geographically, we are the only significant two-ocean power and there is no conventional military threat to our land borders. The American Midwest is the world's largest contiguous farming area and is served by an unmatched water transport system. Water transport costs less than 10% of land transport and we have more navigable internal waterways than the rest of the world combined. The United States has more major ports than the rest of the Western Hemisphere combined. No other country has physical insulation and food surpluses remotely approaching ours. Our continental shale oil and gas resources are more than sufficient for our needs.

JAMES M. DEITCH CPA, CMB

Demographically, we have a sustainably growing population with a reasonable age distribution, far superior to the demographics of Russia, Japan, and China. For centuries we have attracted risk-taking, entrepreneurial, hardworking people and those people and values pervade our culture.

Historically, we have not had a war on our territory for more than one and a half centuries and we have built up an unmatched store of undisturbed infrastructure and capital. Our total debt pales in comparison to our capital and income.

Eddy Perez, CEO of Equity Prime Mortgage and a member of the Board of Directors of the Mortgage Banking Association of America, has a similar worldview:

> *"Everything is possible in America. It's not easy; however, all of your wildest dreams are possible if you believe in yourself, treat people with respect, and work your butt off!"*

None of this is to say the United States does not face risks and challenges. It always has. The greater point is that our advantages allow us the freedom to make mistakes *and* continue to prosper. For long-view strategic planning, the time scale of the United States must be measured in centuries, not decades. And for lenders, the strategic view has to start looking *far beyond the markets currently facing us to the boundless opportunities that lie ahead.*

A HISTORY OF THE INDUSTRY – LEARNING FROM THE PAST

Stan Middleman of Freedom Mortgage often suggests one look at history as a yardstick of where an industry has been and where it might be heading. In research for this book, I was surprised to find that the mortgage banking industry was remarkably well developed in the late 1800s. As you review this short history, note that strategies such as standardization, diversification of funding sources via securitization and whole loan trading, and mortgage product niches were firmly in place 125 years ago. Though technology had not yet emerged, the strategic thought of how to serve customer segments for the good of the customer and the industry were clearly present.

The industry was divided into two segments: "Farm Mortgage Banking" to fund agricultural expansion in the Midwest and Great Plains and "Urban Mortgage Banking," which funded a nationwide trend toward ownership of single-family homes beginning about 1900.[3]

> "Farm mortgage bankers used informal recourse arrangements to ameliorate the risks and informational asymmetries investors faced when purchasing whole loans; these intermediaries did so by developing and maintaining reputations to buy back troubled loans they had originated and serviced, so that their investors suffered no losses.[4]"

It is interesting that the desire on the part of the Farm Mortgage Bankers to protect their reputations by repurchasing non-performing loans protected investors, with the Farm Mortgage Banker

---

[3] Dr. Kenneth A. Snowden, The Research Institute For Housing America; Special Report, 2014, "Mortgage Banking In the United States, 1870–1940."

[4] Dr. Kenneth A. Snowden, The Research Institute For Housing America; Special Report, 2014, "Mortgage Banking In the United States, 1870–1940.", page 3.

JAMES M. DEITCH CPA, CMB

foreclosing on the property and recovering its funds through the subsequent sale of collateral.

> "Urban mortgage bankers, in contrast, developed explicit mortgage insurance products to deal with the same issues. Second, over time, mortgage bankers in both the farm and urban markets found it advantageous to move beyond the "retail" business of selling whole loans by forming long-term, exclusive relationships with life insurance companies.[5]"

> "Finally, mortgage bankers in both sectors experimented with private mortgage securitization, but in different forms. In the 1880s, large western farm mortgage bankers established their own covered mortgage bond programs, and the same innovation was later introduced in the urban market. But after 1910, urban mortgage bankers also began to use participation certificates to combine or divide, and even to create tranches, from the payment streams of specific mortgage loans.[6]"

I was surprised to learn that participation certificates to parse individual loans, as well as a form of a derivative collateralized mortgage security, existed before the Great Depression. Many of these innovations were lost during the Great Depression and did not resurface until more recent times.

What is the relevance of this discussion to today's mortgage industry? This history is important because many of the underlying processes in modern residential mortgage lending had their genesis in these

---

[5] Ibid, page 4.
[6] Ibid.

early urban lending processes. In some ways, the common sense approach to residential mortgage banking of that era has been lost to the mechanistic requirements that resulted from the mortgage crisis of 2007-2009. As Dave Stevens said, "We have a commodity mortgage business run by many leaders who grew up with a business model designed in the 1930s." My colleagues and I discussed the most recent cost data released by MBA as part of the quarterly mortgage profitability survey. The news wasn't good, as the per-loan costs to produce a mortgage ballooned to about $8,800 as of the first quarter of 2018.

It's not just costs that affect the industry. Liquidity and cash flow are equally important.

Stan Middleman of Freedom Mortgage shared his view on liquidity. Stan is looking back to the liquidity issues of 2007-2009 for strategic lessons learned:

> *"We're going to have a few robust periods of growth in the coming several quarters, probably four or five, six, maybe eight quarters before the economy hits the wall a little bit. But liquidity matters.*
>
> *If you don't have a strong servicing asset for cash flow, you've got an issue. If you're retaining your servicing, you're certainly originating with a negative cash number. Independent mortgage bankers don't have typically enough liquidity to run their business. It's going to be really challenging to be profitable in the short run, but combine that with the reality of originating negative cash, your cash expenses are beyond what the MBS execution is, which means that you have to sell the servicing in order to make a cash profit.*

It's an interesting environment. The cash drain on an independent lender is really dramatic. Some companies like PennyMac and Quicken raised debt. These companies can retain servicing. It's going to be increasingly more difficult to go to the capital markets to raise debt. So when those markets shut down, you better have already raised enough debt to support your efforts going forward. So, if I were sitting here today and didn't have enough cash, I would be very concerned."

We are at an inflection point, and some lenders will make a quantum leap to earn superior profitability, outstanding customer satisfaction, and manufacture defect free loans. Some lenders will not.

EXAMPLES OF STRATEGIC LEVERS

This book is about finding the right elements of strategy to win. It's about moving the right strategic levers to positions that allow one to *manage differently* and compete *effectively*. It is about knowing how to earn superior profitability by providing outstanding customer service and to produce defect-free loans.

Pure and simple.

It's about snapping together the correct elements of business process and technology in a way that the company makes a compelling offer to a customer and induces that customer to act in a way that benefits the customer and the company. Ideally, in the words of Rick Bechtel of TD:

"We want to solve a problem for a customer that they may not even be able to articulate. We want to achieve awareness

of customer intent before they act. We want to discover that you are buying a house before you told anybody. Even a realtor.

We'll know you plan to buy a house because we saw you on Zillow, we saw you on the realtor website. We saw that you rented a car in the town you looked at homes on Zillow. We saw that you have a plane ticket from your town to that town.

We think you're buying a condo in Florida. And so, you're going to start seeing us pop up on ads and whatnot. The key is we don't have to advertise to millions of customers. If we can narrow down that list to the 50,000 customers that look like they're going to buy a house this year my ad budget is substantially reduced.

And more importantly, we can start that relationship with a customer through a much less costly direct-to-consumer channel."

To illustrate these concepts, I want to take a moment now to share a personal example of a non-mortgage financial services transaction using the strategic levers of channel of distribution, technological and process transformation, product niches, and diversification of product. See if you can pick out how each strategic lever is used.

I needed to make a five-city trip over two weeks. I used Kayak. com to research itineraries and costs. Several of the flights were on American Airlines, so I jumped onto AA.com to find more details about the aircraft on each leg, as there are specific seats on aircraft that are much more comfortable and have more legroom than others, depending on the aircraft. The phone rang, and the Kayak and AA.Com sessions timed out as I took that call from a client.

As I was speaking with my client, I opened Google to find a resource to help with the discussion. Near the end of the call with my client, while still on Google, an American Airlines ad appeared. It caught my eye, as it offered a specific routing and fare that I had been researching prior to the call. After the call ended, I clicked on the ad and was taken back to AA.com. Immediately, an offer appeared along the lines of this:

"A Citi Executive Platinum credit card can help you retain your American Airline Platinum Status, enjoy premier early boarding, get preferred coach seating at no charge, and work in the airport in the quiet surroundings of the Admiral's Club".

I clicked on the bait.

"You'll earn 75,000 miles and 10,000 Elite Qualifying Miles after you spend $40,000 on the card."

I was struck by the ingenuity of the offer. They know my pain! The next thought was, "How the hell do they do that?" (More on how they do that a little later.)

The application experience involved the following: Name, address, social security, income, acceptance of disclosures, click. Ten seconds later, "Congratulations, you are approved for a $39,500 credit limit and you will receive your card in five days. You can use the card now with a virtual card number."

The next day, I receive a notice from FedEx. The card is being sent overnight, here's the tracking number. The credit line provided was just short of the $40,000 spend needed to earn the 10,000 platinum qualifying miles and the 75,000 'free miles.' Brilliant!

The card arrives as promised, and Citi and American induced me to pay a $450 fee for the privilege of the opportunity to purchase their products.

So how do Citi and American partner to actually use the data to make the offer? This may not be exactly precise, since American Airlines informed me their marketing efforts are proprietary, and 'no' they would not like to be interviewed for my book, but thanks for buying an American Airlines Executive Platinum credit card! Here's informed speculation:

A company named Epsilon may have been at work here. From some research:

> "Companies may come to Epsilon to get more information about their current customers or to obtain information about potential customers who may be interested in their products or services. This information helps make the advertising more relevant and enables a company to send you offers more tailored to the things that interest you. Companies want to find the best fit for their products, and Epsilon helps them determine their optimal target market. This benefits you, as the offers you receive will be more tailored to things you might be interested in. This process also helps companies control costs since they focus their efforts on sending materials to people interested in their products."

Using supplemental data provided by a firm such as Epsilon, American Airlines merged that data with data obtained internally by monitoring my flying habits. American has the internal data to identify that I was *not* on track to renew my Platinum status, as my current travels fit better into Southwest Airlines cities and schedules.

JAMES M. DEITCH CPA, CMB

American received a data feed from Kayak when I clicked on American itinerary presented by Kayak to check out the aircraft on their routes and likely acquired all the city pairs data I was considering.

American also has data that I pay for tickets with an American Express Platinum card. American knows that the AMEX card no longer provides access to Admiral's Clubs, as American inked a deal with Citi to replace AMEX a few years ago. A timely offer is made, hitting all my potential pain points, and I clicked to apply for the Citi Executive Platinum credit card.

Up to that point, I hadn't realized I needed that card. As Steve Jobs, former CEO of Apple, often said, "People don't know what they want until you show it to them." As to the financial services industry, Rick Bechtel of TD's words came to mind, "A strategic leader solves a problem for a customer that they may not even be able to articulate and that the customer will pay to resolve once identified."

So how were the strategic levers used in this example? Citi used the channel of distribution of a partner airline AA.Com. I never explicitly visited Citi's website. Technological and process transformation was snapping together big data, associating that data in a creative way, making it easy to apply and get approved, and following through to make the product available instantly. Product niches offered several different versions of a credit card with features assembled to appeal to a specific segment. The diversification of product snapped together airline benefits and a basic credit card with a hefty fee.

The relevance to mortgage banking is that mortgage lenders have more data about a customer than American Airlines and Citi combined. It's just that mortgage lenders don't use the data as adroitly as AA and Citi.

INDUSTRY CONTEXT

Think about these strategic levers in the context of the many factors affecting the mortgage banking industry that are set out below:

The discussion below expands on how these factors are affecting the industry as a whole:

- High cost to originate is a function of sales costs, regulatory costs, and the increasing documentation burden imposed on lenders.

- New competitors include experienced teams starting a new entity, FinTech start-ups entering the field, competitors, primarily banks, that had reduced their commitment to industry returning to compete, as well as unforeseen entrants that may spring forth; think Amazon, etc.

- Low inventories of homes for sale arise from a variety of issues. New home construction after the 2007-2009 crisis plummeted the and remained below the rate of new family formation since 2007. Zoning and development restrictions have curtailed construction in California, parts of the northeast, and other geographies. "Impact fees" and related infrastructure costs increased the cost to develop land, along with slow approvals and a reluctance of banks to lend on raw land. Low inventories of affordable homes are a subset of low inventories in general. The cost of real estate in the Bay Area, New York City, and other areas is prohibitive to all but the most well-off homebuyer segments.

- Home affordability is affected by rising interest rates, increasing property taxes, some of which are no longer deductible, raising the effective after-tax cost of taxes, rising insurance premiums due to natural disasters, as well as home price appreciation. Home affordability is also adversely influenced by the current Dodd-Frank 'ability to repay' requirements which make it difficult for multi-generational family units and independent contractors, such as Uber drivers, day labor, gig economy workers, etc., to document income and source of assets.

- One can see the big data players beginning to infringe on refinancing opportunities as well as finding ways to skim off the best employees and customers. This begs the question of 'who owns the customer?' We'll visit that topic shortly.

- The regulatory climate has substantially improved under the current administration. The subsiding of the 'regulation by enforcement' climate, regulatory relief to banks in the form of expanded QM, the passing of provisional licensing, the Office of the Comptroller of the Currency moving forward with a 'FinTech' bank charter, and other areas discussed later appear to be very positive developments.

- The "Rocket Mortgage Effect" helps customers demystify the mortgage lending process. The application drives at the heart of some consumer misconceptions, such as one needs 20% down to buy a home. Rocket also has put a premium on speed, as well as increased pressure on margins since any consumer can be preapproved with a rate quickly. Rocket Mortgage lit the fuse on technologically driven services to mortgage customers in a way no other lender has accomplished.[7]

- Consumer expectations are rising, due to the Amazon effect as well as consumer experiences in rapidly getting financed for credit card and auto loans.[8] Why should it cost $9,000 and take 30+ days to get a mortgage?

- FinTech progressed from early efforts focused on the initial consumer interest in a mortgage to application to broader process automation, big data, and transformational opportunities. More effort is flowing into blockchain and big data with the promise of substantially reducing the cost of a mortgage loan.

---

[7] I don't count AmeriQuest's Super Bowl sponsorship or their ridiculously funny television ad campaigns about 'Don't Judge too Quickly' at https://www.youtube.com/watch?v=EHG9-of_WtQ as even remotely similar to Rocket Mortgage's introduction.

[8] Chase internally describes its strategy as 'Digitize Everything'. They are following through with Finn (online only banking services), Roostify for mortgages, Car Shopping and Financing in one app, etc.

RISING INTEREST RATES

The end of thirty years of declining interest rates have likely eliminated refinances as the lifeline that subsidized the industry. Since
2010, $7.7 trillion of mortgages have been refinanced, compared to
$6.4 trillion of purchase lending. Since 2001 the statistics are almost
exactly the same— $21 trillion of refinancing to $16.5 trillion of
purchasing. Said another way, 55 out 100 mortgage transactions
since the beginning of 2001 were refinance transactions.

The refinance business has been a source of business for many lenders since 1981. It was the 'easy money' after the 9/11 attacks and
after the subprime meltdown that fueled the refinance booms and
boomlets. The convergence of many economic factors suggests the
'easy money' period is over. See the long-term trend of mortgage
rates in the chart below:

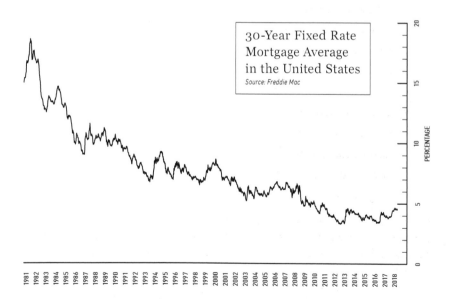

30-Year Fixed Rate
Mortgage Average
in the United States
Source: Freddie Mac

The implication is straightforward— more than half of the historical first mortgage volume of our industry is likely gone for a long time. Eddy Perez commented on the business climate of recent years:

> *"[The industry] sat in a bubble. The bubble was created by refinances. Up until about a year ago, a lot of companies were getting through the slow months with refinance lending. Then margins were exploding in a positive way. It was easy to pay originator compensation.*
>
> *Recently I've heard about originator comp plans that pay 250 basis points! It's just not practical. It's not mathematically possible. Ownership, investors, GSEs, your warehouse lenders expect profitability. However, there are people that are still offering crazy compensation plans that overvalue a loan officer's worth and are trying to justify it. All that's doing is really pricing these competitors out of the market, as margins compress."*

2017 was the first year in the 21st century in which purchase volume exceeded 65% of total mortgage volume. One has to go back to 1999 to get the same 65%. Most of the employees that entered the mortgage banking business in the last 18 years have never experienced this mix of business. Two-thirds to three-quarters of first mortgage originations will be for purchase.

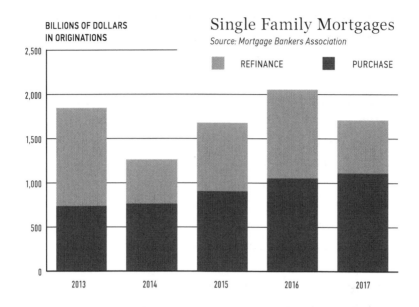

BILLIONS OF DOLLARS IN ORIGINATIONS

Single Family Mortgages
Source: Mortgage Bankers Association

REFINANCE   PURCHASE

My brother, David, is the smartest of the Deitch children. He worked as a foreign exchange trader at major global banks, which took him from Chicago to New York, San Francisco and finally 10 years in London. He made a big career change in 1998, as he saw disruption coming to foreign exchange trading through automation. He moved out of the transactional foreign exchange business to provide relationship management, financial planning and wealth management services to high net worth clients for a leading brokerage firm in North Carolina.

David told me "I'm buying a house in Charlotte. My mortgage is going to be a jumbo ARM product, with the rate linked to one month LIBOR. You may think I'm crazy, but even though interest rates have been falling since the early 1980s, I think they will continue to go lower for a long time. I can withstand some volatility in my mortgage monthly payment."

Thirty-year fixed mortgage interest rates were about 7.5% when David bought his house and followed a long-term trend downward for most of the 18 years David owned his home. During that time, short-term rates were usually well below fixed interest rates. David's analysis proved correct and profitable. David sold his original house in Charlotte in 2017. He purchased a new home close to his office.

We sat on the porch of his new home enjoying a nice French burgundy wine in the early days of the summer of 2018. David reflected on his area of the financial services industry. "I am fortunate to have developed many 15 to 20-year relationships with clients. Clients want good advice from advisors who understand their situation and care about them; who have empathy. Empathy can never be replaced by a robo-advisor. The technology leverages the advisor; it won't replace the advisor." My jab was, "David, you have empathy?" His wife Marie burst out laughing. "With clients, yes. With you, probably not," was his shot back. "Touché!" I responded, in my best French accent.

The mortgage banking industry is beginning to innovate with loan product. Chris George is Chairman-elect of the MBA, and his firm CMG Financial recently offered a LIBOR product innovation offering customers the chance to pay the least amount of interest possible. It's a complex product that requires training and a relationship approach to the customer to ensure that the product is a fit. The discussion of the pros and cons of the product provides the forum to develop rapport and relationship with a client. It provides an opportunity to provide advice to a customer beyond just qualifying for a 30 year fixed rate mortgage.

According to CMG Financial, "The 'All In One Loan' lets a borrower avoid tens of thousands of dollars in excessive mortgage interest, pay-off your home in half the time or less, and gain access to your home's equity dollars without having to refinance." The product is combined with a demand deposit checking account and a first lien revolving thirty year credit line equal to the first mortgage amount. This product is an example of the strategic levers of product niche, diversification and relationship in action. The product leverages technology through an on-line simulator to run scenarios for the borrower to determine if the 'All in One Loan' fits their needs.

The concept that technology leverages a human, but cannot replace human relationship and empathy is a compelling thought. Relationship and empathy are needed before trusted advice can be conveyed. It's why I've included "relationship and empathy" as a strategic lever in mortgage banking. It's an underused strategic lever in the mortgage banking industry.

Marcia Davies amplified these thoughts on building relationship and empathy for both customers and employees:

> *"You really need to take care of people that are working hard to help you advance company objectives. It's your job to make sure that you treat them well and you listen to them and you help meet their needs. As I rose into leadership, sadly my father died very young so he wasn't there for me to get his advice. But I'll never forget that adage to treat people the way you want to be treated. A lot of times you show up with empathy seeking to understand somebody else's point of view. Even when I'm frustrated because you never know what may have happened that morning. And you never know what's going on with someone else.*
>
> *Relationships and empathy are a priority and a key strategic plank. People show respect to one another. Diversity would be considered as something that's required in order to get*

to the best result. And we would really listen and factor in the contributions of the whole team by developing trust and relationship."

In the future, the industry may adopt some of the wealth management model: pay a loan originator for working in the clients' interest over the product life cycles and provide empathy and a trusted advice to the client. That's a big contrast to the loan originators interviewed in the "Big Short," bragging about how much they made selling customers loans based on fraudulent borrower income and asset information. I believe a long-term relationship approach is necessary for success in the purchase market.

The shift toward purchasing business and away from refinances discussed earlier has not been a singular event. The chart below shows the shift:

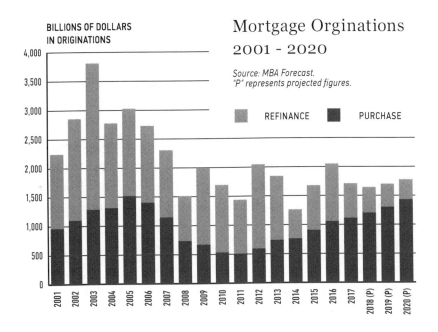

BILLIONS OF DOLLARS IN ORIGINATIONS

Mortgage Orginations 2001 - 2020

Source: MBA Forecast.
"P" represents projected figures.

REFINANCE   PURCHASE

At the same time, customers have seen equity in their homes recover above the peak levels in 2007. The combination of economic growth, absorption of excess inventory from 2005-2010, and continued affordable interest rates have created price appreciation in housing stock. At the same time, the majority of homeowners with a current first mortgage have a fixed rate under 4%, as set out in the chart below:

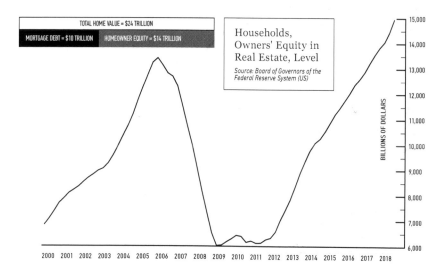

How will mortgage bankers adapt to the expanded levels of customers' equity in their homes, coupled with a rising fixed rate interest environment? Customers' equity exceeds total mortgage debt in the United States. There is no incentive to refinance. But customers will still need to remodel or upgrade their homes. Pay for college. Invest for retirement. *A plethora of opportunities for lenders.*

Jerry Schiano of SpringEQ noted the substantial increase in homeowners' equity and noted:

"Banks will begin to do more [second lien lending] and their product offerings and credit box are expanding. We have some banks talking to us because they want to do more than they could generate themselves. Some mortgage companies will begin to try to figure out how to get more involved in second lien lending. It's just tough because the economics are so different than the first mortgage business, and the revenue levels don't support commissioned loan officers. We're kind of one of the few second lien standalone companies."

Ed Robinson of USAA brings three perspectives for strategic thought:

"Number one, don't think like a mortgage banker. Think like a marketer or customer experience guy. You can't just learn overnight how to service a customer. Number two, really think about how to move the needle when it comes to digital experiences. Don't hesitate to look at what's going on in the Amazons of the world. Zappos, Alibaba, you name it. They are taking customer experience and meeting customer needs before the customer even realize it's a want or a need. Third, really understand the fundamentals of the entire process. Not just sales, fulfillment, or servicing. Learn the entire value chain in the business model because then you can literally parachute in to solve problems holistically or at any one point more efficiently and more effectively than anyone else.

The customer wants transparency throughout the entire lifecycle of the journey. I think about the way that I walk into CVS or Walgreens. We call it the 'shop by use model' [at USAA] which is kind of interesting for a bank to get on that road. You walk in the door of a CVS or Walgreens. You know certain things are up front. You know that there's a wavy aisle that goes all the way back to the pharmacy. The pharmacy lets you pay there or pay up front on your way out. You know what meds to take and when because it's very clear as the pharmacist explains it to you. So, we've got to have that same kind of view across our home buying journey."

Clearly, the industry has changed. The change makes me wonder about loan officers and IMBs in general. My first day of training in 1976 for my new employer at the time, Arthur Andersen & Company, CPAs really drove this point home. Harvey Kapnick, a legendary CPA, started his talk with, "Look around the room... half of you won't be here in two years, and half of you will never pass the CPA test. You have to work differently and much smarter than you have ever before." That advice is just as applicable today, as refinance transactions fall, as it was on a freezing day in St. Charles, Illinois at "Andersen's Boot Camp."

In a discussion about loan officers with Phil DeFronzo of Norcom Mortgage, Phil noted that it's tough for a refinance-oriented loan officer to make the transition to a purchase book of business. I used this anecdote, which left Phil laughing pretty hard: consider a Pilot and a Bus Driver. The Pilot can quickly learn how to drive a bus, but the Bus Driver has no hope of quickly learning how to fly a plane. Refinance oriented loan officers are the bus drivers of the mortgage banking business. We continued the discussion: don't waste your time on any loan officer whose book of business is primarily refinance. If they could do purchase business, they'd already be doing it.

Again, don't waste your time with refinance oriented loan officers. Find new blood and teach them a relationship oriented purchase business model or find seasoned hands with the business mix that fits your model and pay them. Or consider focusing your strategy as well.

OPPORTUNITIES GOING FORWARD

In my 2018 book, "Digitally Transforming the Mortgage Banking Industry," a central theme was 'Begin with the End in Mind'—specifically goals for customer satisfaction, defect-free loans, and profitable, efficient operation. With regards to this, Roy Luo, a consultant with PwC, stated:

> *"Starting with the end in mind for these three metrics made sense. In this book [one] might explore how a lender might find the right balance between customer satisfaction, defect-free loans and efficient operations to yield the desired profit."*

This seems like a commonsensical starting place to my mind, as well. Well-developed strategies should begin with balance, and understanding that 'right balance' begins with evaluating and looking at the disruption facing the residential housing industry.

Next, we'll examine the levers of strategy and develop a model for expressing strategy using those levers. The rest of the book proposes how the levers should be deployed to achieve the objectives of superior profitability, outstanding customer satisfaction, and defect-free loans.

We'll examine the Six Levers of Strategic Intention and examine a variety of Strategic Models for the industry, including a review of half a dozen specific company examples. We'll also look at data-driven strategies to evaluation Products, Loan Officers, Account Executives, Loan Processors, Underwriters, Closers, Shipping, and Secondary personnel. We will then summarize lessons learned from discussions with Mavericks at about Strategic Transformation. Then onto a case study of the application of Strategic Transformation. We'll wrap up with thoughts on Information Security for Mavericks.

CHAPTER 2
DISRUPTION

In the last chapter, I introduced you to my brother David. In 1998, one reason that he made his career change was because he anticipated that the introduction of electronic foreign currency trading platforms would increase price discovery and reduce trading margins. He recognized the disruptive impact of technology on *his job* and reacted by using the investment and risk management skills he had acquired to build a new career.

At about the same time, I had the opportunity to observe real-time, large-scale disruption and get the perspective of someone who studied these ideas. I met Professor Clayton Christensen in 1998 when I was participating as a CEO guest in an innovation workshop at Duke University. The workshop was conducted by Duke University and Professor Christensen on behalf of Nortel Networks to assist the company in plotting a strategy to transform itself from a legacy telecommunications company into a twentieth-century technology competitor.

It was a pivotal time for the company and the stakes were high. Nortel Networks Corporation, formerly known as Northern Telecom Limited, was a multinational telecommunications and data networking equipment manufacturer headquartered in Ontario, Canada. It was founded in Montreal, Quebec in 1895 as the Northern Electric and Manufacturing Company[9]. At its height, Nortel accounted for more than a third of the total valuation of all the companies listed on the Toronto Stock Exchange, employing 94,500 people worldwide.

In 1997, 97% of the households in the United States had a landline telephone connected by copper wire to a wireline telephone company.[10] Today, more than half of current households have no landline phone and only 6% are landline only.[11] At the time of the conference, rapid innovation by companies like Level (3) and Cisco were cutting into Nortel's telephony business. Nortel was in the process of acquiring Bay Networks as a strategic response and the dot.com economy was rapidly expanding.

There was a big shift coming and Nortel apparently had no coherent strategy in place.

Why? There seemed to be little awareness of how disruption can transform an industry. During the three days of the workshop, it appeared to me that the majority of the senior participants had a very difficult time accepting that the legacy wire-line telephony business would be quickly cannibalized. It was equally hard for the senior managers to foresee that connectivity would be democratized away from traditional wire-line telephony providers.

The Nortel executives, as a contrast, appeared frustrated at times that their senior team could not shift its mental model from its legacy business to the opportunities that could be at hand. Dr.

---

[9] www.nortel-us.com

[10] http://www.morrisanderson.com/company-news/entry/the-line-is-dead-the-future-of-telephone-cable-and-wireless-communications/

[11] https://www.theverge.com/2017/5/4/15544596/american-households-now-use-cellphones-more-than-landlines

Christensen privately commented to me that large organizations oftentimes had senior teams very reticent to abandon the legacy models that still appeared to work.

The workshop ended and, in my opinion, the executives seemed even more frustrated at the senior team's desire to find ways to *extend* the life of legacy technology rather than to intentionally cannibalize the Nortel legacy platform in a swift thrust forward. In time, Nortel's business model *was* disrupted. Nortel declared bankruptcy in 2009, unable to shift to a rapidly changing technological environment. It finally died after an eight-year bankruptcy in 2017.

Chris Wattie of Reuters reported that "Judges in Delaware and Canada approved a plan on January 23, 2017 to pay more than $7 billion to creditors of Nortel Networks, ending years of litigation. The rulings by ... [U.S. and Canadian bankruptcy judges] ends one of the longest and most expensive Chapter 11 cases, marked by battles over funds raised by the company's liquidation."[12]

There was a similar disruption in another segment of the telephony infrastructure. American Telephone and Telegraph (AT&T) dominated long-distance telephony. Long-distance calling was based on the distance to the party being called. Rates of $1.25 per minute were common. To this day, AT&T persists with its few wireline customers still willing to pay 'toll charges,'[13] even for local calls. The following is from AT&T FAQ on its website:

What are local toll calls?

---

[12] Reuters, January 24, 2017.

[13] AT&T called these charges 'toll charges,' and I'm told the origin of the term 'toll charge' goes back to the replacement of the 'toll' to ship physical letters and documents via horse-drawn carriage with modern long-distance communication.

Local toll calls span greater distances than local calls but fall short of being long distance calls. These calls may be in your area code or in a different one -- across town, or in the next county. Local toll calls are sometimes referred to as regional toll, shorter distance, local long distance, or, in Hawaii, inter-island calls. You'll generally find these calls listed in the itemized section of your local phone bill. View an illustration and explanation of all the various call types.

The persistence of a small segment of customers, the 6% who still use landlines exclusively, fuels the temptation to assume the current business model will persist. There's actually a business term for this: "Cash cows." Laggards continue to pay for a service long since its disruption. It doesn't cost ATT much to maintain legacy 'local' long distance, and it's a cash cow. A small group of laggard customers will continue to use a service, even into its obsolescence and long after it has been economically disrupted.[14]

This is what the mortgage banking industry needs to understand and understand clearly. Failure in identifying disruption and shifting trends—even if tradition tells us otherwise—will only hurt us as

---

[14] The 1980s were a period of rapid deregulation of a variety of industries, including airlines and telephone service. Microwave Communications Inc. (MCI) took advantage of deregulation and competed with AT&T with a different technology. Instead of copper cables running across the country, MCI used microwave towers to transmit voice communications between points. Other long-distance telephone providers jumped in using fiber optics and voice over internet protocol. AT&T's long-running monopoly on long-distance communications was disrupted and the cost of long-distance telephonic communication fell rapidly.

A recent conversation with a millennial regarding calling across the country via a cell phone illustrated how complete the disruption has been. I asked him what the call from Massachusetts to California used to cost. He looks at me in disbelief. "It's always been free. Why would you pay for a call by the minute? That makes no sense."

JAMES M. DEITCH CPA, CMB

an industry in the end. Loan originators won't be replaced. Their role, compensation, and duties, however, will look vastly different.

Dave Stevens discussed a recent LinkedIn post he made that questioned an overvalued asset, that being of some mortgage loan officers:

> *"It makes no sense to pay a loan officer 120, 150 basis points when the lender ends up with 20 basis points of profit and takes all the risks." "I got a lot of hate mail. I didn't say there was no need for loan officers. What I said was the value proposition for loan officers is broken.*

> *Loan officers who make a couple hundred basis points for a one-time origination without any obligation or risk downstream for performance or duration risk. Loan officers refinance that loan over and over again. That model makes absolutely no sense. If you are building this from scratch, you wouldn't build the model the way it works today. Far too many bodies. Far too much cost. And particularly for sales commissions, it's absurd. What's been paid for someone who is basically quoting four and a half percent and no points. And getting the same documentation that you would get if you went online to Quicken.*

> *It makes no sense to pay 120-150 basis points for what they currently do, which is source transactional business."*

My brother David saw disruption in the foreign currency trading business. It made no sense to pay traders that much money for what they do, either. Now, most foreign currency trading is automated, even at the consumer level. Foreign exchange conversion became a commodity. The cost structure paid by banks trading for currency have been replaced with automation. Most currency traders didn't see it coming. Some currency traders stayed in the foreign exchange business by providing strategy and advice to clients. Those that didn't or couldn't make the switch were forced to move on.

I needed British pounds for a trip this summer to Scotland. My bank offered currency via its website. Get a quote on dollars to pounds. Compare the exchange rate on Bloomberg to ensure the rate was competitive. Place the order. The British currency is delivered overnight by FedEx.

DISRUPTION DEFINED

Why is disruption so hard to identify and act upon for so many industries? The term "*disruption*" in its current usage was likely coined by the very Harvard professor I met on that 1998 panel, Clayton Christensen, in his 1997 book, "The Innovators' Dilemma." Christensen described his book as "focusing on 'disruptive technology'. The book shows why most companies miss out on new waves of innovation. Whether in electronics or retailing, a successful company with established products will get pushed aside unless managers know when to abandon traditional business practices." Most of all, according to Christensen, "Disruption is a process, not an event, and innovations can only be disruptive relative to something else."

Stan Middleman of Freedom Mortgage speaks of 'bad historians' who fail to look at history to learn lessons going forward. Stan commented that executives frequently do not see the disruption coming in an actionable sense. Don't worry, we'll drill in on disruption in the mortgage banking industry in a moment, but for now, let's look a bit more at disruption across industries.

Consider disruption in the 1900s in the transportation industry. The New Yorker magazine carried an interesting, and perhaps bawdy, look at disruption at the turn of the century in 1900.[15] Author Elizabeth Kolbert states, "This story—call it the Parable of Horse-shit—has been told many times, with varying aims." Kolbert writes:

> *"In the eighteen-sixties, the quickest, or at least the most popular, way to get around New York was in a horse-drawn streetcar. The horsecars, which operated on iron rails, offered a smoother ride than the horse-drawn omnibuses they replaced. New Yorkers made some thirty-five million horsecar trips a year at the start of the decade. By 1870, that figure had tripled.*
>
> *The standard horsecar, which seated twenty, was drawn by a pair of roans and ran sixteen hours a day. Each horse could work only a four-hour shift, so operating a single car required at least eight animals. Additional horses were needed if the route ran up a grade, or if the weather was hot. Horses were also employed to transport goods; as the amount of freight arriving at the city's railroad terminals increased, so, too, did the number of horses needed to distribute it along local streets.*
>
> *By 1880, there were at least a hundred and fifty thousand horses living in New York, and probably a great many more. Each one relieved itself of, on average, twenty-two pounds of manure a day, meaning that the city's production of horse droppings ran to at least forty-five thousand tons a month. George Waring, Jr., who served as the city's Street Cleaning Commissioner, described Manhattan as stinking*

---

[15] Elizabeth Kolbert, "Hosed", New Yorker Magazine, November 9, 2009.

"with the emanations of putrefying organic matter." Another observer wrote that the streets were "literally carpeted with a warm, brown matting . . . smelling to heaven." In the early part of the century, farmers in the surrounding counties had been happy to pay for the city's manure, which could be converted into rich fertilizer, but by the later part the market was so glutted that stable owners had to pay to have the stuff removed, with the result that it often accumulated in vacant lots, providing breeding grounds for flies.

The problem just kept piling up until, in the eighteen-nineties, it seemed virtually insurmountable. One commentator predicted that by 1930 horse manure would reach the level of Manhattan's third-story windows. New York's troubles were not New York's alone; in 1894, the Times of London forecast that by the middle of the following century every street in the city would be buried under nine feet of manure. It was understood that flies were a transmission vector for disease, and a public-health crisis seemed imminent. When the world's first international urban-planning conference was held, in 1898, it was dominated by discussion of the manure situation. Unable to agree upon any solutions—**or to imagine cities without horses** [my emphasis]—the delegates broke up the meeting, which had been scheduled to last a week and a half, after just three days.

Then, almost overnight, the crisis passed. This was not brought about by regulation or by government policy. Instead, it was technological innovation that made the difference. With electrification and the development of the internal-combustion engine, there were new ways to move people and goods around. By 1912, autos in New York outnumbered horses, and in 1917 the city's last horse-drawn *streetcar made its final run. All the anxieties about a metropolis inundated by ordure had been misplaced."*

Few people saw the transformation of transportation in the major cities from horse-drawn carriages. Henry Ford didn't try to disrupt urban transportation. It just happened as a result of the automobile.

It can be difficult to envision a way through disruption and its paradigm shifts. Many in the mortgage industry can't envision a future where the production cost of a mortgage loan is $1,000 or less and the commitment happens in minutes. But we can learn from disruption in other industries. Before we drill in on disruption in the mortgage industry, let's look at how disruption occurred again in the transportation industry, and how another disruption in the urban transportation industry quickly, and seriously, affected the financial services industry.

FINANCIAL SERVICES DISRUPTION

More recent disruption in the transportation industry led to the failure of several financial institutions in New York State. If anything, these examples show just how quickly disruption can transform an industry.

Uber arrived on the scene in 2015 and ridership of Yellow Cabs fell precipitously. New York City as well as Chicago, Boston, Philadelphia, and other cities regulate cab hailing[16] via "taxi medallions."

---

[16] Cab hailing means flagging down a cab on the street as opposed to going to a cab stand or calling a taxi company to send a car. Cities regulate cab hailing ostensibly to protect citizens from unscrupulous 'gypsy' limo drivers and potential criminals. Cities also regulate cab hailing as a source of licensing revenue.

The increase in competition and its impact on New York Yellow Taxi ridership is evident in the chart below. Uber's ridership surpassed the New York Yellow Taxi ridership in May 2017. This feat was accomplished in under three years. Other ride services such as Lyft, Juno, and Via have entered the New York market to capitalize on Uber's market expansion success.

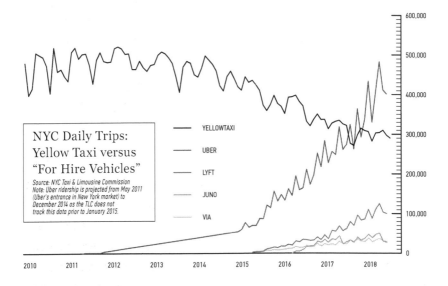

NYC Daily Trips:
Yellow Taxi versus
"For Hire Vehicles"

Source: NYC Taxi & Limousine Commission
Note: Uber ridership is projected from May 2011
(Uber's entrance in New York market) to
December 2014 as the TLC does not
track this data prior to January 2015.

The increase in competition has benefited the New York consumer; the total number of individuals using a form of ride services, in the form of a yellow taxi or other for-hire vehicles, has increased as shown in the chart below.

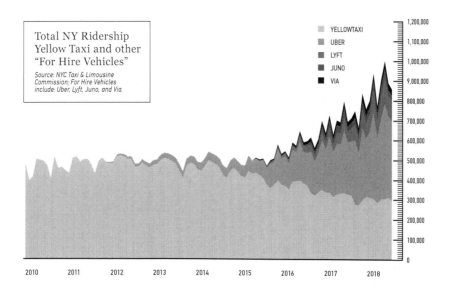

Total NY Ridership
Yellow Taxi and other
"For Hire Vehicles"

Source: NYC Taxi & Limousine
Commission; For Hire Vehicles
include: Uber, Lyft, Juno, and Via.

YELLOWTAXI
UBER
LYFT
JUNO
VIA

1,200,000
1,100,000
1,000,000
9,000,000
800,000
700,000
600,000
500,000
400,000
300,000
200,000
100,000
0

2010 2011 2012 2013 2014 2015 2016 2017 2018

There is a direct and opposite correlation between Yellow Taxi ridership and taxi medallion prices, whose value is dependent on the cash flow streams generated for the driver from rider fares. Fewer riders taking Yellow Taxis equates to less income from fares and tips collected by the taxi drivers. This ultimately depresses the demand and prices for taxi medallions. Its negative impact on New York taxi medallion prices is illustrated below. New York has two classes of taxi medallions – individual and corporate. Note: Trend lines were added for certain months as there was limited to no sales transfer activity.

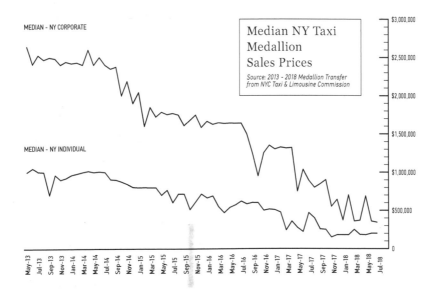

MEDIAN - NY CORPORATE

Median NY Taxi
Medallion
Sales Prices

Source: 2013 - 2018 Medallion Transfer
from NYC Taxi & Limousine Commission

MEDIAN - NY INDIVIDUAL

In the past, Credit Unions and other financial institutions originated loans secured by these taxi medallion assets. They viewed them as lower risk loans largely due to the stability and continued upward appreciation of the taxi medallion prices to back these loans. For years, prices of taxi medallions escalated, just like home prices through 2006. Then, Uber...

The sudden change in the ride services landscape changed the status quo. Financial institutions holding loans backed by taxi medallions faced a dilemma – the $1,000,000 loan that they originated and hold on their balance sheet is now backed by an asset worth $200,000. What if the borrower decides to stop paying, such as in strategic default, or is unable to make payments on the loan due to the decrease in monies collected from fares? The impact has been and continues to be significant and widespread. The table below shows those financial institutions no longer in existence as a result of carrying these assets.[17]

---

[17] These financial institutions failed. Many others suffered large loan losses due to the depreciation of medallions but did not fail.

INSTITUTION NAME	HEADQUARTERS	DATE CLOSED, LIQUIDATED, OR PLACED INTO CONSERVATORSHIP	ASSET SIZE IN DOLLARS (AT TIME OF CLOSING)
Montauk Credit Union	New York, NY	September 2015	162,000,000
Melrose Credit Union	Briarwood, NY	February 2017	1,700,000,000
LOMTO Federal Credit Union	Woodside, NY	June 2017	236,000,000
First Jersey Credit Union	Wayne, NJ	February 2018	86,000,000

Source: FDIC

My early experience with disruption discussions with Dr. Christensen still ring true: "Figure out if you were a competitor, how would you kill off your business?" The last twenty years have provided many examples of disruption. One disruptor stands out: Amazon in the book distribution business. And in the publishing business... and the retail products business. And the music distribution business. And in the cloud hosting business. And in....? Seems like Amazon could keep going ad infinitum at this point.

Other examples? Blockbuster Video's physical videotape and video disc rental model was disrupted first by a mail-order competitor Netflix. Netflix then disrupted itself, and advanced the bankruptcy of Blockbuster, by streaming content. Apple Music disrupted the major music publishing and distribution system by offering downloads via the iPhone and then cannibalized iTunes by adopting a streaming model. Apple now is being disrupted by other streaming services.

DISRUPTION IN MORTGAGE BANKING

How is disruption manifesting in the mortgage world? Speaking on the topic, Brian Stoffers, Vice-Chairman of the Mortgage Bankers

Association and CBRE stated that:

> *"We have enormous strategic decisions to make, which will shape our future. The impact of technology disruptors and the financial implications they have on our decisions is incredible...Technology helps us be more efficient and effective with our very limited time in a fast-paced business world.*
>
> *"Homebuyers want more efficient, instant home buying information, but they still want in-person assistance as well. Technology has given homebuyers the ability to be as self-sufficient as they would like. They can even bypass traditional realtors using sites like Zillow and Redfin."*
>
> *Rocket Mortgage "completely changed the mortgage lending landscape forever by appealing to consumers' appetite for online gratification and turbocharged the desire for every other lender to better serve their customers."*

When researching for this book, I developed the following hypothesis about disruption from a *consumer's* standpoint:

> **Disruption occurs when a better solution becomes so obvious and so easy that it becomes ubiquitous.**

Amazon is so easy that its been adopted by all age groups. It's not a technology, it's a tool of everyday life. It's ubiquitous. Here's the proof:

Age Cohorts of Amazon Prime Users

Source: comScore and Business Insider

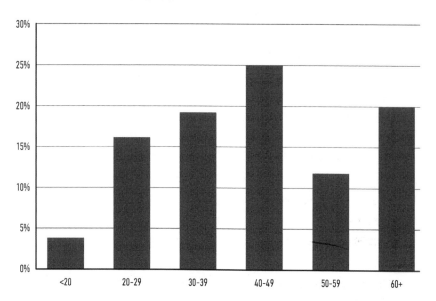

I purchased a home in Florida and virtually all the things needed to equip the new home were available and delivered to my door by Amazon. It never occurred to me to physically 'go shopping' in Naples for kitchen appliances, dishes, glasses, a wine fridge, linens, etc.

Disruption continued as I became a 'wire cutter.' No need for a landline in the Florida house. Why pay for something so expensive and limited when a cell phone works so much better and there is no such thing as 'long distance toll charges' or 'local long-distance toll charges?' No need for cable TV, too, as Fubo works anywhere, anytime and costs less than cable.

With this in mind, consider this corollary to my hypothesis from a *business* standpoint:

> ***Your business model works until it doesn't.***

YOUR BUSINESS MODEL WORKS UNTIL IT DOESN'T

Taxi medallion lenders, Blockbuster Video, Borders Booksellers, Nokia, etc. Their business model worked until it didn't. So, what about your business model for mortgage banking?

According to the MBA, the typical mortgage banker spends $8,000 to manufacture a loan. To a degree, the existing mortgage banking ecosphere was insulated during the last ten years by the financial crisis. The GSEs and FHA were literally the only game in town for thirty-year fixed rate mortgages that met 'Qualified Mortgage' guidelines. Regulators and especially the litigious CFPB maintained the status quo with 95+% of loans having a government guarantee of some sort, as well as layering thousands of dollars per loan in compliance costs. There really wasn't an imperative to reduce costs, since all lenders had the same product and the same regulations.

Steven Schwalb, CEO of Angel Oak, believes product innovation will disrupt the mortgage market of the next several years. Steven and I had a discussion on the future of the GSEs and the innovation Angel Oak is bringing to the mortgage market:

> *"We originate high-quality non-QM loans that don't fit into the GSE credit box. We innovate by using full-documentation criteria to qualify loans but use data that doesn't fit neatly into the GSE box. The demand for our product is expanding, and our knowledge of the value chain from touching the customer to delivering high-quality loans to the private label, mutual fund, and other non-GSE investors is tightening the spread of our products to the GSE execution. Our customers benefit, as do we."*

I related to Steven a conversation I recently had with a GSE executive. The GSE executive asked how competitors might compete aggressively with the GSEs. My reply was that the guarantee fees of GSEs make no sense compared to the losses in the 2012-2016 vintages. Virtually no losses, but 40-45 basis point guarantee fees collected on a pristine credit book.

Here are the economics that show FannieMae has collected about $30 billion in aggregate guarantee fees from 2012-2016 for the loans guaranteed by FannieMae. The unpaid principal balance of defaulted loans is $781 million, not billion. 3.3 basis points of total principal balance guaranteed at issuance. This is my calculation and assumes prepayment speeds etc. but the economics are materially the same. There are guarantee fees of about 40 times defaulted balances and the defaulted balances are unpaid principal, not actual realized losses. No wonder the jumbo/conventional spread is negative!

YEAR	PRINCIPAL BALANCE ($MILLIONS)	DEFAULT UNPAID PRINCIPAL BALANCE ($MILLIONS)	LOSS RATE (DEFAULT DIVIDED BY UPB)	APPROXIMATE CUMULATIVE GUARANTEE FEES COLLECTED ($MILLIONS)
2012	608,103	300	0.049%	10,946
2013	483,419	246	0.051%	7,070
2014	310,374	152	0.049%	4,190
2015	421,057	72	0.017%	4,263
2016	540,409	11	0.002%	3,648
Total	2,363,362	781	0.033%	30,117

Source: Fannie Mae Statistical Summary Tables including HARP: July 2018

Several executives stated that the GSEs have noticed that they are selling higher balance, high credit quality loans away from the GSEs and into the private label and whole loan markets. The GSEs are said to have relayed that they expect a 'representative mix' of the lender's loan production. They don't want 'adverse selection'.

Yet their pricing model has no relation to the credit risk of a large segment of loans sold to the GSEs.

Guess what? We are approaching the inflection point of when the GSE business model will work, until it doesn't. Those lenders that contemplate a much smaller market share for the GSEs will prosper. Those who don't will see continuing margin compression.

I also mentioned that the handwriting is on the wall. I'm writing this paragraph on September 6, 2018, ten years to the day since the conservatorship of FreddieMac and FannieMae. I had lunch a while back with James Lockhart, former CEO of the Federal Housing Finance Agency, the regulator of the GSEs. The lunch was on a prior anniversary of the conservatorship. I asked him, upon reflection, what it was like to take the GSEs into conservatorship. Jim said:

> *"Liquidity and confidence were rapidly flowing out of the GSE marketplace. A month before the conservatorship, GSE execs were in denial. The events of late August and early September created the unthinkable. The GSE business model doesn't work anymore. There was no choice. Temporary conservatorship was the only choice."*

Ten years later, the jumbo to conventional loan spread is negative by 10-15 basis points, according to Mike Fratantoni, Chief Economist of the MBA. That tells us that the GSE guarantee has little value versus trusting the credit box of a jumbo seller. Ten years prior, according to Mike, the spread was a positive 50-80 basis points. The GSE business model worked until it didn't. Only legislative and regulatory gridlock keep both GSEs alive.

Steven Schwalb confirmed my thinking: "We can buy high-quality loans that could go to the GSEs, but our investors provide a better execution." In short, companies like Angel Oak will compete for the high-quality end of the GSE loan spectrum, squeezing the GSEs between an emerging comfort with high quality loans from private securitizers and the FHA credit box.

Private mortgage insurance companies are willing to move beyond the GSE business. Patrick Sinks, CEO of MGIC, noted that "As the private label market matures, it takes a greater understanding— a common understanding— among the parties as to what the risks are in the way you [transfer credit] risk and what that could mean. [If a transaction is credit enhanced,] we place great emphasis to make sure that our [master] policy is crystal clear. That a lender understands exactly when we will pay our claim and when we won't. And there is also a great drive not only for clarity and transparency but uniformity."

For lenders, a word of caution: "If a lender focuses largely on conventional GSE lending, they are going to be crushed," Steven Schwalb asserts. "The margin's not there, and it's a commodity. And it's going to get worse before it gets better."

RELEVANT PARALLELS

As readers may have noticed so far, I frequently study parallel industries to get a sense where mortgage banking might be headed. Equity stock trading, including its mechanics and cost structure, is particularly noteworthy.

Charles M. Jones, of Graduate School of Business Columbia University[18], studied the history of stock commissions. Stockbrokers

---

[18] A Century Of Stock Market Liquidity And Trading Costs; Charles M. Jones, Graduate School of Business Columbia University, First version May 22, 2002.

used to function in much the same behavior patterns as mortgage loans officers. Stockbrokers would earn their licenses and then be turned loose to prospect for clients. The stock brokerage business was transaction based. Find a customer, provide them with some ideas to trade stocks, make a commission on each trade, and build a book of transaction-based business.

For example, prior to Schwab Discount Brokerage and SEC regulations in 1975 enabling discounted commission, commissions for stock trades were fixed. As Jones wrote, "Trading 100 shares of [a $40] stock would result in a 'one-way' commission of $39, or 0.975% of the money involved. One-way meaning either to buy or sell a stock. The 'round trip' of buying and then selling a stock would have commission paid on each end of the round trip.

"During this era, the NYSE commission schedule was always linear: a trade of 3,000 shares incurred a commission 30 times as large as a trade of 100 shares. Thus, one can think of commissions as a proportional tax on transactions, where the tax rate depends on the share price.[19]"

The stock brokerage commission rates were similar to current loan officer compensation. The commission rates are similar and linear: the larger the loan balance, the larger the commission. Sales commissions make up between 40 and 60% of origination costs, according to MBA data.

What happened to this paradigm in equity stock trading? Currently, an individual can trade 100 shares of stock for about $5.00. Brokers are no longer compensated by trade size. Mutual funds and Index funds reduced the transaction costs for consumers even more. The

---

[19] Ibid.

industry transformed itself away from transaction fees and towards fee-based investment management advice based on account size. The better the account performs, the more compensation for 'registered investment advisors.' (Note the name change – no longer 'brokers' but rather 'advisors.') Annual fees of .20% to 1.00% of funds under management are common with no specific commissions or costs to trade. Interestingly, account 'churn,' buying and selling similar stocks, has fallen dramatically.

My brother David summed it up: "Your industry (mortgage banking) remains totally transactional. That's where large wealth management firms were 25 to 30 years ago. Of course, there are some situations where if a client wants to buy and hold a security; they should just pay the one-time transaction charge. But paying an asset-based fee on more actively managed assets often benefits the client, because clients pay for results rather than for activity.

People often focus on the idea that when the client makes more money, the advisory revenue increases. That is true, but what is more important is that the advisory revenue decreases when the client's account value decreases. So the advisor needs to both minimize losses and maximize gains. Their revenue and income depend upon it. When I pay for advice, I want the person providing advice to have lots of skin in the game, too. I think that helps create durable trusting relationships.

Susan Stewart, CEO of SWBC Mortgage, commented on the relationship versus transactional elements of mortgage banking:

> *"[Building that relationship with a customer] is a great idea because once you help a buyer into a house, then we know them. We can use our customer relationship management or the servicing relationship to continue to build a relationship*

with them and be there the next, and the next, and the next time they buy a home. We'll be the lender for them."

The former brokerage industry transformed itself into the wealth management business and away from transactional services into relationship-based services. Residential finance needs to do the same thing.

DODD-FRANK'S IMPACT OF PERPETUATING EXCESSIVE ORIGINATOR COMPENSATION

Dodd-Frank attempted to correct perceived and actual abuse of customer by loan officers steering the customer to unsuitable but high commission products. Mortgage banking has been a transaction-oriented business since the 1870's when agents were commissioned for originating agricultural farm loans on the Great Plains.

Dodd-Frank removed the incentive for higher commissions based on loan terms. A laudable goal. Well-intentioned regulation to prevent 'steering' has effectively put a floor on originator compensation, to the detriment of the very consumers the regulation purportedly protects. Prior to Dodd-Frank, originators were at risk of reduced compensation or loss of compensation if a loan was mispriced, incorrectly originated, or did not meet quality standards of the lender. Originator compensation regulations prohibit compensation from being tied to loan terms.

Intended to prevent 'steering' to higher priced, and higher commissioned, subprime loans, the regs also prohibit a lender from holding a loan officer accountable for mistakes in pricing, borrower data, etc. The regs also make compensation design a difficult task. A

$100,000 first-time homebuyer with some degree of credit blemishes in need of significant structuring assistance must have the same commission rate as a $450,000 refinance for an 800 FICO 60% LTV borrower. The impact is a $1,100 commission for a borrower that needs a capable loan officer that can structure, versus a $4,950 commission on the refinance. In actual practice, the excessive retail refinance commission mandated by Dodd-Frank, no commissions based on loan terms, including purchase or refinance, or degree of difficulty structuring the loan, generally drives refinance customers to an online lender with a low per-transaction compensation plan. The same goes for jumbo loans.

BANKS MAY BECOME MORE FORMIDABLE COMPETITORS

Recent changes by Congress that expanded the Qualified Mortgage imprimatur to any mortgage loan funded by a bank with less than $10 billion of assets may change the calculus for portfolio lending by mid-sized banks. The loan has to meet Ability to Repay but is otherwise a QM loan.

How many banks have less than $10 billion of assets? 4,160 banks in the US, not including credit unions and mutual banks not insured by the FDIC. The makeup of banks, by asset size, is as follows:

Banks by Asset Size
Source: FDIC

More than a trillion	4
More than 100 billion	26
More than 10 billion	104
More than 1 billion	630
More than 100 million	3,530

That's a lot of new potential lenders interested in the safe harbor of QM that can now originate QM loans without meeting GSE documentation guidelines. According to Dave Stevens, that may take some time. "Bankers are still shell-shocked from the regulatory onslaught from the crisis. The risk appetite just may not be there for a lot of banks".

Federal legislators are beginning to react to the difficulties brought on by Dodd-Frank. Kenneth Harney, the syndicated columnist writing in the Washington Post on September 5, 2018:

> *"Say you're a Lyft driver and you run a cash-intensive food truck business on the side. You earn good money and you have decent credit scores and savings, but your income jumps around from month to month depending on sales. You're likely to have a hard time convincing lenders about your total income — it's not steady, and at least some of it can be difficult to document. Your loan officer may end up saying: Sorry, I can't fit your income pattern into the boxes mandated by federal qualified-mortgage (QM) regulations, so I just can't do your loan.*
>
> *Enter the "Self-Employed Mortgage Access Act," co-sponsored by Sens Mark R. Warner, D-Va., and Mike Rounds,*

R-S.D. It would expand lenders' permissible sources to verify incomes beyond the relatively narrow range specified in current federal QM regulations. According to Warner, as many as 42 million Americans — roughly 30 percent of the workforce — are self-employed or in the gig economy."[20]

It's ironic that ten years after the GSE conservatorship, it takes an act of Congress, literally, to fix an obvious flaw in the overall mortgage market.

Disruption in Demographics and Housing

The demographics of population, housing stock, and business climate have a large bearing on the housing market, housing affordability, and opportunities available to mortgage lenders. As discussed above, the positive lift from refinance originations will be much less of a factor over the next few years, compared to the prior seventeen years.

Homes for sale inventory is tight and nationwide inventories are at about a five-month supply. The months' supply is the ratio of houses for sale to houses sold. This statistic provides an indication of the size of the for-sale inventory in relation to the number of houses currently being sold. The months' supply indicates how long the current for-sale inventory would last given the current sales rate if no additional new houses were built.

---

[20] https://www.washingtonpost.com/realestate/mortgage-investors-want-to-make-it-easier-for-gig-economy-workers-to-get-loans/2018/05/29/082e7eb2-634b-11e8-a768-ed043e33f1dc_story.html?utm_term=.89016ef4ca8c

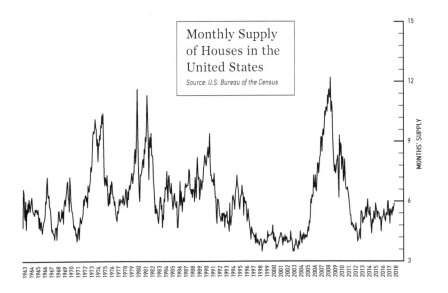

Monthly Supply
of Houses in the
United States
Source: U.S. Bureau of the Census

The Washington Post reports that according to the National Association of Realtors' latest data, the total listings of homes for sale are down by 8.1 percent over the past year alone, and they have fallen year over year for 33 consecutive months. A new study by Trulia found that inventories have sunk to their second-lowest level since the company began tracking them in 2012. Meanwhile, prices are up in major segments: median starter homes by 9.6 percent for the year, trade-up homes by a median 7.5 percent.[21]

The age of housing stock continues to advance, according to the National Associate of Home Builders.[22] Less than 20% of the current housing stock was built since 2000, and 53% was built prior to 1980. This means a growing need for rehabilitation financing, as well as construction financing for new homes.

---

[21] https://www.washingtonpost.com/realestate/shortage-of-houses-for-sale-reaches-epidemic-levels/2018/03/26/f7020f26-311a-11e8-8bdd-cdb33a5eef83_story.html?noredirect=on&utm_term=.630d637d8e17

[22] http://eyeonhousing.org/2017/01/the-aging-housing-stock-3/

JAMES M. DEITCH CPA, CMB

Share of Owner-Occupied Housing
by Year Structure Was Built

Source: National Association of Home Builders

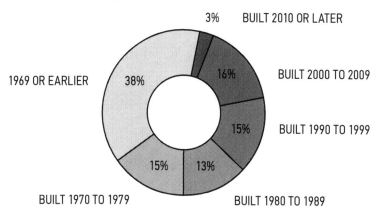

3% BUILT 2010 OR LATER

16% BUILT 2000 TO 2009

1969 OR EARLIER 38%

15% BUILT 1990 TO 1999

15% 13%

BUILT 1970 TO 1979 BUILT 1980 TO 1989

For a quick look at the effect of the political and tax climates on the housing market, take a moment to reflect on a survey by Chief Executive Magazine. Chief Executive readers rate each state as the 'Best and Worst States for Business,'[23] based on state taxes, state regulation, workforce quality and degree of education, and living conditions, including housing stock availability and affordability, etc. Interestingly, California, which ranks 50th as the Worst State for Business, saw a net outflow of talent from the Bay Area. About 12,000 residents fled San Francisco in 2016, and the net outflow for 2017 climbed to 25,000. Nor is the future prognosis particularly great. Seventy-four percent of millennials in the Bay Area are currently considering an exit, according to the Urban Land Institute.[24] Housing prices are such that the California Association of Realtors now suggests a $181,000 income is necessary to purchase a home, more than 3.5 times the national average.[25]

---

[23] https://chiefexecutive.net/best-worst-states-business-2018/

[24] https://chiefexecutive.net/young-talent-leaving-silicon-valley/

[25] Ibid.

Chief Executive Magazine State Ratings

	BEST STATES 2018		**WORST STATES 2018**
1	Texas	50	California
2	Florida	49	New York
3	North Carolina (Tie)	48	Illinois
4	South Carolina (Tie)	47	New Jersey
5	Indiana	46	Connecticut
6	Tennessee	45	Massachusetts
7	Georgia	44	Oregon
8	Colorado	43	Alaska
9	Arizona	42	Washington
10	Ohio	41	Hawaii

A state's business model works until it doesn't. Connecticut is now experiencing the impact of its high-tax, difficult business climate. Speaking at a summit convened by Connecticut governor Dan Malloy, Jim Loree, CEO of Stanley, Black & Decker, opened the meeting with a sprawling diagnosis of Connecticut's fiscal ills as reported in the Hartford Courant on January 9, 2018:

> *"In 2001, Loree said, Connecticut was ranked the eighth-most competitive state in the country by the Beacon Hill Institute, 'competitiveness' being a measure of fiscal policy, quality of life, labor supply and infrastructure. By 2016, he said, Connecticut had slipped to 43rd by the same index.*
>
> *Outmigration is a well-documented phenomenon in Connecticut, but Loree singled out a telling statistic: On average, a family that moves into Connecticut has a household income of $93,000. The average income of a family moving out is $123,000. With such a fluctuating tax base, Connecticut's income stream is "incredibly volatile," Loree said, rendering*

*the state "very vulnerable to market downturns." A dispro-
portionate amount of tax revenues flow from a handful of
well-heeled enclaves, he added. Thirty-six percent of the state's
personal income tax revenue comes from 10 towns, including
West Hartford, Glastonbury and Fairfield County towns.
Twelve percent of all personal income tax comes from 357
families alone, Loree said."*

Demographics, state friendliness to business, and state tax burdens all impact the inflows and outflows of potential homeowners. These macroeconomic factors matter as much as the level of interest rates to homebuyers. And lenders have to factor in the strategic impact of these demographic and macroeconomic changes.

FAMILY FORMATION DEMOGRAPHICS AND CULTURAL CONSIDERATIONS

You may remember Samir from "Digitally Transforming the Mortgage Banking Industry." As a quick summary, I learned during an Uber ride in New York City that Samir was married and appeared to be in his late twenties or early thirties. This new acquaintance of mine was a first-generation immigrant working hard to build his dream in the U.S. He was saving money. His dream included buying a home of his own for his family. He said, however, he wasn't sure he could get a loan for a home. I wondered how I would qualify him for a mortgage if I were a loan officer.

Family formation is perhaps the strongest driver of the economy, as it generates the need for shelter, transportation, and furnishings, among other things. Family formation is largely driven by demographics, which are propelled by births and immigration, as well as the time dimension.

Since more than half of family formations will likely be by minority households and/or with non-traditional earners seeking to purchase a home, meaning not W-2 employees, how does one serve these borrower cohorts?

Patty and Rick Arvielo stress that any inroads into minority homebuying communities need to focus on culture, not ethnicity. This is the kind of high-touch topic that betrays the weakness in automation. As the Arvielos frame it, we need to underwrite to culture and "You can't automate that." While addressing minority needs is now an industry-wide conversation, the industry is still not ready for it. As Bill Cosgrove put it, "The industry talks out of both sides of its mouth on this issue. While we all know that minority ownership is not where it should be, many of the rules are still lined up against those loans falling into place."

Patty commented,

> "The difference between the Hispanic borrower and the non-Hispanic borrower is that there is a trusting cultural need. That trust is generally nurtured face-to-face. So, I think at the end of the day, any buyer, regardless of culture or ethnicity, is going to be starting their home buying process on the internet or their phone. But virtually all home buyers want to have a relationship with their loan officer, whether it's face-to-face or otherwise.
>
> To build that relationship, the number one issue is education in the Latino market. Latinos are a broad group and come from different countries such as El Salvador, Guatemala, Nicaragua and Mexico. The home loan process in those countries is very different. They don't have a banking system in those countries that they trust. So, they come into our country first generation, still not trusting the system."

JAMES M. DEITCH CPA, CMB

Some borrowers don't fit the current product set for other reasons. Phil DeFronzo recalls many situations where a "make-sense" loan cannot be done within a GSE context: a divorcee with 60% cash down payment from a divorce settlement, but no income currently, a doctor with a contract in hand from a hospital but who hasn't started working yet...the list goes on.

Jamie Korus-Pearce, Nathan Burch, and others recall many instances of borrowers that don't meet the specific technical requirements of an investor but nonetheless appear willing and able to repay the loan as agreed. According to Nathan, "Underwriting judgment has been eliminated by regulations and punitive enforcement." Jamie recalls when it was possible to grant "common sense" underwriting decisions based on the judgment of a skilled underwriter. We need to return to that time.

Taking the long-term view on this issue is essential. As Billy Beane put it in our discussions, reframing his organization's view of the value of certain assets over time was the crux of implementing transformation at the A's, and also took its cue from another thought leader—Warren Buffet himself. "Warren Buffet has a long term view, and seeks undervalued companies that will outperform over time... That's our strategy. We look for undervalued assets." In my view, undervalued assets in mortgage banking include intent to develop a durable relationship oriented strategy, and strategy to integrate the technology stack towards big data and relationship management.

HOUSEHOLD FORMATION

These issues cannot be ignored, given the sizable shifts on the horizon. The following chart shows family formation over a 50-year period.

Average Annual Household Formation

(in thousands)

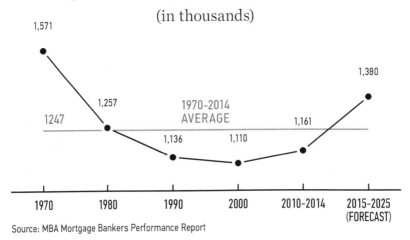

1,571

1,380

1,257

1970-2014
AVERAGE

1247

1,161

1,136

1,110

1970   1980   1990   2000   2010-2014   2015-2025
(FORECAST)

Source: MBA Mortgage Bankers Performance Report

Demographic projections show that roughly 70% of the growth in households from 2015 to 2025 will take place in minority households, a significant change from the past twenty years.

Total Household Growth 2015 - 2025

(in millions)

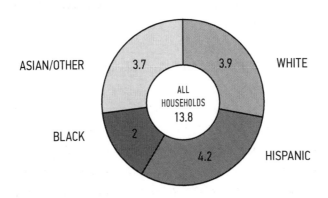

ASIAN/OTHER   3.7   3.9   WHITE

ALL
HOUSEHOLDS
13.8

BLACK   2

4.2   HISPANIC

Source: The Harvard Joint Center for Housing Studies

JAMES M. DEITCH CPA, CMB

The estimate of 2015-2025 family formation of about 1.4 million units per year contrasts with the relatively low rate of new housing construction of 500-600,000 units over the previous ten years.

High-cost areas such as the California Bay Area, New York City, Los Angeles, and other areas have regulatory limits on new construction. Regulatory limitations hit builders particularly hard in the form of impact fees, land density requirements, zoning requirements, and land costs. Add the time required to transform raw land to "approved, improved" land ready to build, and one can see the squeeze on homebuilding, particularly at the entry level. As a result, many families, whether a family unit of one or many, currently rent a home.

Kevin Pearson stated:

> *"The price of housing has made it difficult on new construction for our products. It's hard to increase first-time homebuyer product going forward. Regulatory requirements add $50 to 80 thousand to just getting each building lot ready to build a house on. Thus, it's hard to build entry-level housing in many locations, since the cost of land drives the total home price above 'entry level'."*

And according to Julie Piepho of Cornerstone:

> *"New housing stock is affected by land availability, the cost of building, the lack of skilled construction labor, and the cost of permitting. We've also got the myth of the 20 percent down payment requirement. We have to help customers find and document the source of down payment for a 5% down loan, and show the customer that it can be done."*

Patty Arvielo noted that Hispanic borrowers "are very family oriented and culturally the family unit is supreme." It is not unusual to have three or more generations in one household[20]. This cultural trend does not fit neatly into easy access for credit on several dimensions. First, not all potential homebuyers fit neatly into a credit score-driven credit model. Patty noted that family ties will often result in intergenerational and familial financial assistance needed by one family member.

This cultural benefit doesn't translate into a dimension of Dodd-Frank Qualified Mortgage and Ability to Repay regulations. Nor does it serve immigrants who may not have established a scorable credit history but are industrious and earning.

Ten years after conservatorship, U.S. Senators Warner and Rounds are working on a bill. The non-QM market, meanwhile, is beginning to function well without any federal assistance, and with less federal threats of regulation by enforcement.

About eight years ago, a dozen CEOs, including me, visited with Consumer Finance Protection Bureau (CFPB) Director Cordray to speak about QM and safe harbor. Director Cordray expressed shock that lenders would be slow to venture into non-QM. I presume his shock was genuine. Over the last eight years, continuous efforts by the industry – including by former MBA CEO Dave Stevens – have swayed the current administration to reduce Mr. Cordray's 'regulation by enforcement' paradigm. The resignation of Director Cordray capped an industry effort to encourage responsible regulation with bright lines of permissible activities.

The resurgence of responsible innovation in the non-QM space makes the Product Niche strategic lever much easier to use for transformation. Many of the leaders I spoke with encourage responsible, bright-line regulation. The non-QM market features full documentation and minimal layered risk.

One CEO had an interesting perspective. "As an industry, the subprime lenders and Wall Street ran amok and created a mess in the real estate finance market. Many of those players failed. That's partially our fault for not policing ourselves. Few of the guilty were prosecuted for their acts. That's the fault of the federal government. The Obama Administration appointed Director Cordray. He stepped in and began to shoot the innocent and push the market towards total domination by the GSEs and FHA. Thank goodness he resigned and will now focus his destructive energy into just one state, instead of the entire country."

As Julie Piepho of Cornerstone noted, not all family formations and millennials aspire to homeownership. The needs of renters are equally important in considering shelter needs. Some of the needs are driven by the economics of geography. Mobility also plays into the decision to rent. A home in the Palo Alto area that seems large enough for two children is $1.6 to $2.5 million. The transaction costs[21] into and out of a home approach 10%, or about $160,000-$250,000. The likelihood of employment mobility and the high entry cost in many locales drives many millennials into renting for a period of time—perhaps for a long time. But not always.

Speaking of millennials, Patrick Sinks, CEO of Mortgage Guaranty Investment Corporation, shared this story:

> *"I have a 26- year-old in Minneapolis who just bought a condominium. The rent got to be too high, so the thinking is, 'Gosh I'm going to buy a condo.' All the things we've been reading about millennials are not true in all cases. She bought a condo and did it the way millennials go about the*

process. Mobile technology. So, I think it starts with [lender] acceptance that one has to meet the customer on their terms. I think it's an understanding of the technology. It's having some foresight as to where disruption can happen."

Cody Pearce of Cascade notes that many families seeking affordable shelter may rent or purchase non-traditional home units such as manufactured housing. In many high-cost and remote locations, manufactured housing may represent the best option for shelter for a family unit. Cascade has undertaken a business model to serve these clients with affordable and fast financing for non-real estate loans, i.e. chattel loans, meaning the loan is not real property but rather is titled by the state motor vehicle department. Mr. Pearce shared aggregated, anonymized credit data characteristics of targeted market customers with me; the borrower profile with respect to credit score and DTI would fit into the GSE credit box, but the collateral does not easily fit. Nonetheless, Cascade provides a manufactured housing homeowner the ability to own his or her home—just not the land underneath the home.

The answer to these issues is innovation in strategy, product, and in the credit box. But don't wait for the GSEs to solve the issues. Serving the underserved minority and millennial segments extends far beyond the GSE product set.

As discussed herein, family formation will drive the non-QM, non-depository lenders. These lenders have begun to innovate and non-QM product is receiving greater acceptance and tighter spreads to GSE pricing. Banks with less than $10 billion in assets can also innovate, meeting ATR but relaxing the onerous income documentation guidelines of the GSEs.

DISRUPTING THE REAL ESTATE COST STACK

Mortgage banking is not the only industry that is ripe for disruption in the housing market. The cost stack paid by the buyer of a home includes the real estate commission, mortgage costs, both explicit fees and fees paid through elevation of the interest rate, title insurance charges, government transfer taxes, mortgage stamp taxes, and other fees. It's well over 12% of the purchase price of a home. This level of transaction cost may hold back many a borrower, whether they are a millennial, minority, or just about any other borrower. With loan real estate appreciation running 4-5% per year, the breakeven for transaction costs in a home can be three years.

The typical under 30-year-old employee changes jobs four to six times in the first ten years of their career. Transaction costs are the likely reason homebuying is being deferred by millennials, not a lack of desire to own a home. Transaction costs in the Bay Area for a first time homebuyer are crazy. My son looked at homes in the Bay Area and realized a fixer-upper would run $1.5 million. The transaction costs in and out in a three-year ownership period would run almost $300,000. No thanks! Even for a $250,000 home, below the median selling price in 2017, the transaction costs run over $30,000.

Costs for a $250,000 House

Cost Item	Fees	Costs
Realtor Commissions	6.0%	15 000
Mortgage Loan Cost to Originate	4.0%	10 000
Title Insurance and Related Costs	1.0%	2 500
Appraisal, Inspections, etc.	0.5%	1 250
Real Estate Transfer Taxes, Stamps	2.0%	5 000
Total	**13.5%**	**33 750**

This cost stack is paid each time a house changes hands and the fees are largely based on the purchase price, not on the effort required by the providers. I'm sure the following discussion will cost me some friends in the real estate sales and brokerage business and the retail loan officer space, as discussions on 'value add' and 'disruption' invariably mean someone's ox is being gored.

The real estate commission and sales commissions based on purchase price or loan amount are almost counter-intuitive. It often takes more effort to do a first-time homebuyer's mortgage than a $400,000 refinance, yet retail loan originator commissions are by law the same rate. It often takes more effort to sell a first-time homebuyer property than a million dollar trade up home, but the real estate commission rate, usually 6%, is often the same or similar.

The real estate commission 'sides' – the 'listing agent' or sell side, and the 'selling agent' or buy side— are split, generally 50/50. As in mortgage banking, the individual realtor commands most of each side from the brokerage. The real estate sales market is protected by state regulations and an aggressive industry lobbying function. It's the same for the title agent and title insurance market.

Let's also consider the work being performed by the labor elements in the value chain:

- The real estate listing agent provides market knowledge and insight regarding pricing a subject property. The listing agent applies judgment and conducted agent open houses to generate interest from selling agents. In some cases, the agent 'stages' the home. Today, video tours of a subject property substitute for selling agent walkthroughs. Comprehensive neighborhood assessments of schools, tax rates, shopping, and more are available online. The value addition of the listing agent is being diminished.

- The selling agent takes prospects through initial financial qualification, property identification, neighborhood analysis, and physical walkthroughs of the properties. The agent helped buyers complete offer paperwork, though technically the selling agent had dual agency representing the seller. Virtually all of these functions can be completed online, except for the walkthrough of properties.

- The appraiser is a licensed realtor with appraiser qualifications. The appraiser inspects the property, confirms dimensions, and reviews the multi-list service to find comparables to value the subject property. Technology can do all of that with a deeper dataset.

- The title agent performs or supervises manual title searches and prepares the deed and settlement sheet. The actual title insurance is provided by a title insurance company that generally receives 10% or less of the total title insurance charges imposed by the state approved title insurance rates. Much of the title process can be automated.

- The loan agent or loan officer qualifies the borrower, counsels the borrower on loan programs, prepares the application and stewards the application through to closing. We know that much of the process can be automated.

The elements of the cost stack that are ripe for disruption by technology are very broad; notwithstanding government licensing requirements and related lobbying interests that interfere, for the time being, with disruption. Also, consider that the participants in this cost stack rarely have capital or liability at stake in the transaction, they are simply transactional costs. By the same token, customers want advice and are willing to pay a reasonable fee to obtain it. But 12% all in of the purchase price? I think not.

One example of a potential disruptor in the realtor space is Redfin. Redfin, an alternative to traditional real estate, offers sellers a different value proposition. There are other 'flat fee' or reduced cost real estate listing alternatives to the traditional realtor. Redfin appears to have a scalable model that appeals to the consumer, via the look and feel of their website and Redfin's value proposition:

> *"The Redfin business model advocates for the customer. Redfin real estate agents are paid on your review of our service—not just commission—so we're accountable to deliver a good result. On average, homes listed with Redfin sell for $3,000 more and are 6% more likely to close within 90 days than comparable homes listed by other brokerages. Redfin Agents charge a 1%-1.5% listing."[26]*

Another disruptor is OpenDoor. According to The Economist:

> *"Instant buyers such as OpenDoor try to do to property sales what Billy Beane did to baseball. Just as the Oakland A's substituted software for conventional talent scouts, 'i-buyers' such as OpenDoor replace real estate agents with algorithms that crunch data on everything from the number of bedrooms to local crime rates to estimate what a property should sell for."[27] Then OpenDoor buys it at a discount, makes some improvements and sells it. The seller gets a quick sale, albeit at a discount after OpenDoor fees.[28]*

---

[26] Redfin.com

[27] "Fixer Uppers", The Economist, September 15, 2018.

[28] Ibid.

The purpose of this chapter is to explore disruptive opportunities in residential real estate because the whole cost stack seems too high, or the process takes too long. For specifics, we'll look at mortgage banking in particular.

Rick Arvielo, CEO of New American Funding, stated:

> *"The millennial borrower is going to expect a different experience. And I think our industry has to be prepared to deliver. Millennials are used to getting answers in real-time. They're used to self-serving and they're used to being able to push a button and get an answer.*
>
> *That's where I think the breakdown is more likely to occur with mortgage bankers because they're just not in a position to offer that real time experience. So, we spent the last three years developing technology. To really empower the practitioner at the street level, to be able to deliver that kind of service levels by pushing everything right to their mobile device. And then from a marketing standpoint, you know what they are thinking about. It helps build the relationship."*

Brent Chandler, founder and CEO of FormFree, has views on the cost stack in mortgage lending. Like how to completely disrupt it:

> *"FormFree's vision is to eliminate unnecessary friction on the lending process. AccountChek was the first product. It lets a lender access asset balances for a customer's bank accounts without having to provide physical bank statements. My early work progressed to a revolutionary product developed in concert with FannieMae – Day 1 Certainty, or 'DIC'.*

*DIC led to a very innovating product that reduces lenders'
costs by obtaining directly sourced data that can be trusted.
When FannieMae introduced DIC, people literally cheered."*

Jonathan Corr, CEO of Ellie Mae, discussed DIC:

*"Day 1 Certainty is an evolution of really what started off
[the expanded value of direct access to trusted data. It's
the follow-on to] the initial products such as Early Check,
LQA for FreddieMac, and so forth. It's taking the checks
and balances and pushing them very early in the process.
Building in quality from the beginning. That much less
rework. You're going to lower your costs, contract the time
to deliver [a completed loan]. A lender also gets some relief
on elements of representations and warranties."*

Nima Ghamsari of Blend sees the power of a data-driven process:

*"How do you make this a more data-driven process? Instead
of documents, the data will be the thing that's backing the
underwriting decision and not documents long term. And
that will allow for greater efficiencies. And this is where
I think the AI machine learning capabilities will start to
come to bear. In understanding. Not just the underwriting
rules and guidelines but what the consumer behaviors are."*

Brent Chandler sees continued disruption along the lines of Nima
Ghamsari:

*"There's more to come. Game changers. What if we could
provide 'six pillars' of any consumer's credit real time?
Assets, Identify, Liens and Judgements, Credit, Income, and
Employment. With one authorization from the customer?*

The future is using data to eliminate the need to spend time and money documenting assets, income, and employment using 1930's methods."

Brent's vision is more at hand than may be immediately apparent. Maylin Casanueva, Chief Operating Officer of Teraverde, noted:

"It's not just borrower data and ability to pay that can be data-driven. The GSEs and a large number of service firms have data regarding real estate transactions, chain of title, appraisal data, multiple listing service data, real estate tax data, satellite mapping of collateral, neighborhood school, crime, and related data. In short, aside from a human walking through the home to confirm physical condition, the entire home buying and financing process could be done electronically."

Farfetched? In 2015, I purchased a home in Naples, never having physically set foot in Naples until the day I executed the contract. The mortgage application was done online with the builder's mortgage company. The property search was carried out online. We physically spent about four hours looking at a few properties to confirm the condition and to confirm the neighborhood characteristics.

I flew to Naples to settle the property seven weeks later. Did the realtor and builder sales agent really earn their commissions? The loan agent? I provided everything necessary to approve the loan at application submission. Only state barriers to consumer choice prevented me from negotiating the real estate commission and title fees to a level commensurate with the value provided.

Recall my thesis: *Your business model works until it doesn't.* We may be rapidly approaching a time where a whole series of businesses and services in the real estate sector will be disrupted because the customer is exposed to a better solution, one that becomes so obvious and so easy that it becomes ubiquitous.

I worry about Uber, Amazon, Apple, and others becoming possible disruptors in the lending and real estate businesses. Uber did not intend for or plot the failure of financial institutions. The financial institutions were collateral damage to Uber's disruption of urban transportation.

The critical question is this: how can we, as an industry, adopt strategies to 'disrupt ourselves' before someone else does it to us?

CHAPTER 3
HARNESSING DISRUPTIVE FORCES

Having identified disruption in our industry, the natural next step is devising a strategy on how to harness these disruptive forces to a lender's advantage.

While researching for this book, I often thought of my discussions with Billy Beane of the Oakland Athletics. Those discussions reminded me of another movie about sports that relates directly to our current topic of disruption.

Jerry McGuire— played by Tom Cruise in that well-loved film of the same name— confronts a demand from his football playing client: "Show me the money!!" In one famous scene, Cruise shouts again and again "Show me the money!" in an attempt to show his client that he does have the killer instinct he thinks is necessary to succeed as his agent in the industry[29]. Labor costs drive the National Football League, and any savvy player (or agent) knows this. Like the National Football league, mortgage bankers spend *a lot* of money on labor cost.

[29] For those who may not remember "Jerry McGuire," or were too young to see it, here's the clip worth viewing: https://www.youtube.com/watch?v=mBS0OWGUidc

Most manufacturers have a relatively low labor content in their products. Depending on the industry, labor content could be as low as 5% of revenue. The mortgage banking industry's labor content is over 60%, sometimes as high as 70%. It's hard to scale when labor is such a large component. Outsourcing overseas simply reduces the cost of the labor, not the total hours of labor within a loan.

It costs $8,100 to create a new mortgage loan, with just $172 spent on technology. That's just seven to eight basis points of revenue, and far behind the approximately 230 basis points in compensation per loan, according to MBA data. Many lenders in our business suggest technology spending is a major component of their operational costs.

The facts do not necessarily support this thesis. Personnel costs still top 200 basis points of cost or more. Does technology spending constitute a major spend component for lenders? The following is a graph of technology spend by type of lender over time. Technology spend is a relatively small component of the cost of origination, less than 2% of total loan revenue. This equates to 4–8 basis points of cost per loan. Does this mean lenders are underinvesting in technology? I believe so since the labor content of the total cost remains so high.

Technology Spend (in bps) by Lender Type

Source: MBA Mortgage Bankers
Performance Report

BASIS POINTS

2012	4
2013	5
2014	7
2015	5
2016	5
2017	5

BANK

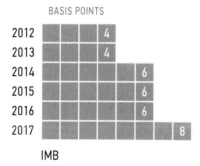

BASIS POINTS

2012	4
2013	4
2014	6
2015	6
2016	6
2017	8

IMB

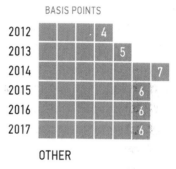

BASIS POINTS

2012	4
2013	5
2014	7
2015	6
2016	6
2017	6

OTHER

COST OF ORIGINATION

Tim Nguyen, CEO of BeSmartee, had some interesting observations on the challenges of cost to produce, labor content, and lender profitability:

> *"In the competitive landscape where Loan Officer compensation is really a big cost, more than a third of the cost is originator cost. When you look at the Stratmor Group numbers, I think 60 or 70 percent of the cost goes out to the originator. It's tough to differentiate yourselves, to compete Lenders' incentive to drive that cost down hasn't truly been there."*

When Tim said, "Lenders' incentive to drive that cost down hasn't truly been there," I did a double take. More than 90% of the loans closed in 2017 ultimately were funded by GSEs or FHA/VA. Lenders just accept that this is the cost structure of doing these loans.

Someday, we will wake up and read that a lender has reduced the cost of originating a loan to $1,000. That will be a difficult moment. Not going to happen? The first steps have already occurred. Disruption is afoot.

Quicken has not only leveraged technology in a transformative way in our space, but also has made sure that the consumer is aware that tech is digitally transforming access to mortgages. Since Quicken's launch of Rocket Mortgage and its Super Bowl launch advertisements, borrowers can clearly see that online options for the completion of a mortgage are available.

Ed Robinson of USAA believes lenders need to be able to support customer interest in a mortgage regardless of how the customer approaches the lender: "Whether it's the web, or if we bought a lead, or if they are a bank customer, the customer feels the same experience regardless of entry point. We have to make sure that that experience is the same across the continuum, and it really comes down to integrating data and offering an omnichannel experience [of the customer's choosing]."

There are more market share opportunities as new construction takes a larger role in the purchase mortgage market. Deb Still of Pulte Mortgage notes that none of her loans are originated by commission-based loan agents:

"Pulte Mortgage uses an affiliated builder business model. Our lead generation comes from the parent company's business, and we offer the value of "one-stop" shopping

to the consumer. We have a fulfillment center, and our origination function aspires to offer the best product, price, relationship and experience to our homebuyers. Our loan officers are not on commission. We pay a base salary and offer incentives for outstanding performance in capture rate, customer service and quality. We do this because our originators are not actually sourcing the business.

You could argue that builder affiliates and other affiliate relationships were the very first consumer-direct models. Today, Pulte is still unique because we've centralized everything, including the origination function and use technology to facilitate the application and manufacturing processes.

Studies show that consumers prefer the convenience of a "one-stop" shopping experience. In recognition of this model, Zillow and other realty firms have recently announced they're entering the mortgage business. Much like other affiliate models, the realty companies are trying to package the sale of the home and the sale of the mortgage."

Many envision technology as empowering the loan officer. As Tim Nguyen put it:

"People will always talk to a loan officer. It is our job to make that easier. It makes the loan officer more efficient. Technology is not the end all. It's simply a platform... the process, the people, the core values come into play... technology has to be done in a way that supports the consumer but doesn't leave them out to be all by themselves."

Stan Middleman of Freedom Mortgage had an interesting perspective on FinTech in the mortgage industry. Rather than driving innovation, Stan feels the industry will need to function essentially as an early adopter of GSE technology, such as Day 1 Certainty and Single Source. Any innovation, he believes, has to start there.

Mr. Middleman continues:

> *"I think it's important to recognize one fundamental fact— in the United States, the government fundamentally finances 95 percent of all homeownership... Fannie and Freddie are actually starting to compete in terms of technology. As that starts to change, I think we'll be forced to be most effective as early adopters, rather than innovators.*
>
> *As long as the government is going to subsidize housing finance, the driver of the technological improvements will be the agencies. And the companies that are gathering up the servicing for those agencies are going to be, I think, the beneficiaries of that activity."*

The fact that technological innovation is required and long past due in the mortgage industry is clear to many. As Bill Emerson put it, "All one has to do is take a look at the millennial generation and the way that they consume information and the way that they interact to realize that if we don't embrace technology as an industry we are going to get left behind ... it would be a shame to see experienced mortgage lenders lose market share because they were too slow to adopt what's right in front of their face."

One way in which the technological innovators in the mortgage industry are addressing this is by developing ways to have the consumer actively managing his or her data as opposed to just *providing* his or her data. While this is transformative in many ways in that it unifies the front-end process, getting accurate data with integrity proves difficult.

JAMES M. DEITCH CPA, CMB

As Tim Nguyen put it, "The more you empower consumers, the more accurate data has to be, because you can't sit there and filter everything and do everything for the consumer anymore. The more power the consumer has, the smarter those tools have to be. It's about managing the data, not providing the data. We want to turn you [the customer] into a data verifier, not a data provider."

This issue—the fact that LOs still dominate when it comes to volume—may account for some of the cultural resistance from some in the mortgage industry to FinTech. It's true that some people just won't change. There is a very successful loan officer I know who still takes an application with a pen. She refuses to use technology, saying simply, "It gets between me and the customer." Rather than adapt, her employer puts up with it because "she sources good FHA business."

LENDER WARS

Skirmishes around this disruptive result have already broken out: Housing Wire carried this headline on August 15, 2018: "Quicken Loans accuses United Wholesale Mortgage of waging smear campaign in battle for borrowers."[30] HousingWire reported that C2 Financial would discontinue offering Quicken Loans' products to clients, alleging that the latter would keep the customers' refinancing to themselves, instead of returning the business back to the former.

Jay Farner, the current CEO of Quicken Loans, stated via email to HousingWire:

[30] https://www.housingwire.com/articles/46479-quicken-loans-accuses-united-shore-mortgage-of-waging-smear-campaign-in-battle-for-borrowers

"In the past year, since the inception of BRAWL, Quicken Loans Mortgage Services (QLMS) has doubled its market share by sticking to what we're best at: providing competitive pricing, industry-leading client service, and always meeting the needs of our broker partners.

We have also received calls of support from partners who recognize that, despite its stated goals, 'BRAWL' is nothing more than a front for a middleman wholesaler who is threatened by the current dynamics in the marketplace. It's clear this initiative is a self-serving, smear campaign driven by United Shore Mortgage and its CEO Mat Ishbia, targeted at its largest competitors. Ishbia is obviously becoming increasingly threatened by the tightening margins of the current market and several larger, better-capitalized competitors who handle every aspect of the mortgage, from origination through servicing.

At the end of the day, mortgage brokers and their customers benefit from lender competition. It's a shame when a middleman who suddenly is feeling the heat of a competitive marketplace resorts to propping up so-called 'industry trade groups' based on a false narrative and made-up circumstances that do not exist to scare some brokers away from doing business with his competitors based on his libelous propaganda."

United Wholesale shot back this statement, also published in HousingWire:

"As the wholesale channel continues to thrive, even in this down mortgage market, brokers now have a stronger voice and leverage to only work with lenders who are looking

for a true partnership. With that resurgence, mortgage brokers are fighting back against lenders who are just in the wholesale channel to build their retail business long term.

This has become a hot topic in the industry over the last 12 months, as the business practices of Quicken Loans and other large retail lenders trying to compete in the wholesale channel have been exposed nationally.

UWM has no issues with Quicken Loans specifically, but does have an issue with any lender that solicits mortgage broker customers and does not treat those brokers as real business partners, and Quicken Loans seems to fit that bill from all the data that is publicly available. UWM is the fastest growing overall mortgage lender in the country, the #1 wholesale lender in America for 3 consecutive years, and will continue to be the biggest advocate for all mortgage brokers across the country."

The fight for who owns the customer will become more acute. A broker finds the customer, does the paperwork, and contractually releases the servicing of that customer, and the cash flows that result over time, to the purchaser of the loan and servicing. The owner of the servicing expects to have that loan on the books 3-7 years to justify the investment in Mortgage Servicing Rights.

The broker is transactionally oriented and contractually releases the servicing to the lender/servicer. This is the same argument that loan officers present over "their" customer. This skirmish is the beginning of the strategic transformation from a transaction-based mortgage banking system to a relationship-based mortgage banking system.

THE MORTGAGE AS PART OF ASSET ALLOCATION

Many wealth managers view a mortgage as part of an asset allocation strategy. It's a source of funds to be managed in the context of a customer's financial planning. A mortgage is an alternative way of buying a home versus paying cash. My brother, David's view is that a mortgage is just a financial instrument similar to a mutual fund, stock, bond, or private equity fund.

This view works currently in a wealth management context. Schwab clients are offered a mortgage loan with Quicken, money center banks view jumbo lending as a wealth management customer acquisition method, and so on. This holistic view is now applied to higher net worth individuals. It's just a matter of time until it percolates throughout other customer segments.

My view is that the winners will:

- Provide the customer with a close personal relationship through a combination of human interactions, artificial and augmented intelligence, and a holistic view of the customer's financial picture.

- Be proactive in providing the customer with suggestions about opportunities and offers that may be in their best interest.

- Nurture referrals from the customer to other customers that the lender might be able to help.

There is a role for relationship-based lenders, no matter what the business format. Lenders with access to their own funds, such as banks and independent mortgage bankers, may have an easier transformation since the ability to act as a principal rather than a broker is a strategic advantage. Banks with portfolio products can innovate more quickly than an independent mortgage banker. Owners of servicing have access to the customer during the mortgage loan's life, as well as the ability to monitor the customer's credit status.

Lenders that don't have these strategic advantages may be able to form relationships with banks and servicers to build a relationship-based model.

The fight for customers may well turn into a protracted war. In the end, the customer may have their own opinion: I'm owned by no one. The lenders that proactively build the relationship mortgage banking model with outstanding customer service will prosper. One thing is clear: the lending landscape of the future will *not* be transaction - based, generating 400 basis points of revenue for each mortgage.

FINDING UNDERVALUED ASSETS: MONEYBALL

Let's look now at how a professional baseball team keeps its payroll cost at less than 25% of the large market teams, and about 40% of the league average while oftentimes contending in its division. Their story is *not* just about lower salaries. It's also about how team strategy and technology intertwine to produce wins at one quarter to one half of the cost structure of other Major League Baseball competitors.

In the script for "Moneyball[31]," Billy Beane is discussing strategy with a fictional character, Peter Brand. Brand is a fictional

---

[31] "Moneyball" is a movie from Columbia Pictures directed by Bennett Miller and written by Steven Zaillian and Aaron Sorkin. The movie is based on the Michael Lewis book "Moneyball: The Art of Winning an Unfair Game," published in 2003.

character based on Beane's actual assistant general manager, Paul DePodesta.

The setting is the team offices, a few weeks after the Athletics loss to the New York Yankees in the 2001 American League Division Series. Due to team budget constraints, 2001 season star players Johnny Damon, Jason Giambi, and Jason Isringhausen will be lost to free agency. How will the Athletics be able to assemble a competitive team for the 2002 season within the Athletics' limited budget? Peter Brand utilizes a data-driven empirical analysis of baseball statistics that measures players in-game activity known as Sabermetrics[32]. The scene goes as follows:

> PETER: There is an epidemic failure within the game to understand what's really happening. And it leads people who run major league teams to misjudge their players and mismanage their teams. They're still asking the wrong questions. People who run baseball teams still think in terms of buying players. Sorry to say that. The goal shouldn't be to buy players, what you want to buy is wins. To buy wins, you buy runs. You're trying to replace Johnny Damon. The Red Sox look at Johnny Damon and they see a star worth seven and a half million a year. When I look at Johnny Damon, I see an imperfect understanding of where runs come from.

---

[32] Statistical analysis has been around as long as baseball has been played competitively. Long before Moneyball became a worldwide phenomenon in the 21st century and before Bill James' baseball writings gained mainstream popularity in the 1980s, Hall of Fame manager Earl Weaver was using index cards to fine-tune his platooning system and pitching changes with the Baltimore Orioles in the 1960s, while Branch Rickey hired statistician Allan Roth in the 1940s to evaluate player performance with the Brooklyn Dodgers. From Society for American Baseball research at https://sabr.org/sabermetrics.

BILLY: And because players have been overlooked because they don't rise to the standards of traditional baseball thinking, we believe that in this river, there are fish...fish who--

PETER: Forget the fish. In this room [we have data on] every available player at every level of professional baseball, and somewhere in that group are 25 players that everyone has else has thrown out. An island of misfit toys. In this room is a championship team that we can afford.

As we discover later on in the movie, it's not just about recruiting overlooked talent. It's about providing the data-driven analysis to make the most of these players. To help the players and managers collaborate on how to get on base, score runs, and win games, an approach that was entirely disruptive in 2002.

The story I related in an earlier chapter about my brother seeing disruption coming is not unique. David saw the future of currency trading and knew that technology moves ever forward. The same mentality towards FinTech should be leveraged when considering the future of mortgage banking. An ever-increasing number of consumers are expecting more advanced interactions and a more streamlined, technological process in the consumer experience. More to the point, and more salient to our search for a streamlined industry, however, FinTech is essential for mortgage banking as an effective tool and one that can help ameliorate the enormous cost and complexities of the loan manufacturing process.

Gordon Moore of Intel introduced an observation that became known as "Moore's Law": the capability of a microprocessor will double every 18 months, given a constant cost. Mortgage lending costs just keep escalating and are not delivering more value for the higher cost.

This is just crazy. There's no other way to describe it. I'll make a bold prediction: in the next three years, the cost of originating a mortgage loan will fall by more than half. If one can't find a way to keep pace with that prediction, I suggest you won't be originating mortgage loans.

Which brings us to disruptive technologies.

Geoff Colvin[33] presented a talk entitled "Leading Ahead of Disruption." My takeaway from the talk was that one should use technology to do low value-added things that humans could do, such as processing loan documents, and focus humans on high-value things that technology can't do, such as building a personal connection to a customer.

Afterward, I had a discussion with Geoff. He said, "Most businesses and products can be disrupted by technology. To find areas that are difficult to disrupt, ask yourself, 'What are humans most driven to do?' It's to build relationships. To have empathy. To engage in creative problem solving as a group. To collaborate." This is why Relationship and Empathy function as a Strategic lever.

Let's review what technology can disrupt the lending process. Could a lender originate and close a first mortgage loan in one day, for under $1,000? As I said earlier, my thesis is that your business model works until it doesn't. Businesses are usually not disrupted by a 'big bang.' They are disrupted when innovators snap together existing pieces of technology and process in an innovative way.

A key point: disruption comes when innovators think, "That makes no sense. *This* is a better way." Note that the innovator doesn't think "There's got to be a better way." They think, "This is a better way,

---

[33] Geoff Colvin is Fortune's senior editor-at-large and has written hundreds of articles for the magazine including its popular column 'Value Driven.' He has written two books, "Talent is Overrated" and "Humans are Underrated."

JAMES M. DEITCH CPA, CMB

and here's how I can do it." Mavericks usually see it coming, but many business leaders don't see it until it's upon them.

DISRUPTION "FALSE POSITIVES"

There are also many disruptive "false positives" in business— a purported game-changing innovation that it is said will revolution- ize the business that doesn't deliver on its promise. An example is automated underwriting.

The promise of automation in mortgage banking first appeared on the horizon in 1995. My mortgage banking company had the privilege to work as a beta tester on both Desktop Underwriter (DU) and Loan Prospector (LP). I was looking forward to a streamlined mortgage process. Our company was an initial roll-out lender for LP in 1995, and in 1996 tested an early, very early, it turns out, ver- sion of collateral assessment for LP that was subsequently scratched.

LP arrived with great fanfare and promise. According to Leland Brendsel, former Chairman and CEO of Freddie Mac, "Fred- die Mac's automated underwriting service, Loan Prospector, *has fundamentally transformed the way mortgages are originated.* [My emphasis] With Loan Prospector, approving mortgages is easier and faster, costs are lower, and the application of objective underwriting criteria is more consistent. Additionally, by more accurately mea- suring risk, Loan Prospector extends the benefits of the mortgage finance system to more borrowers."[34]

---

[34] Leland C. Brendsel, Chairman And Chief Executive Officer, Freddie Mac, before the Subcommittee On Capital Markets, Securities and Government Sponsored Enterprises Of The Committee On Banking And Financial Services, U.S. House Of Representatives, May 16, 2000.

We all know that promise was never fulfilled, and we know why. LP and DU have, in fact, *augmented* the mortgage underwriting process that has been in use since the federal government got involved in mortgage banking in the mid-1930s.

Twenty years after the launch of LP and DU, the FannieMae and FreddieMac Selling Guides exceeded 1,000 pages. LP and DU didn't disrupt the industry because they did not *fundamentally transform the way mortgages are originated*. It isn't a lack of technology or reliability that is holding either back.

These systems are hamstrung because they have to exist within the context of the written underwriting guidelines and documentation standards from the 1930s. The GSEs are inoculated against significant and fast innovation due to their historical legacies, the political elements of the federal housing regulators and federal legislators, and the burden of conservatorship. It's safe to say we can expect only incremental change from the GSEs.

The GSEs will be the disrupted, not the disruptor. Again.

This is not without precedent, of course. The GSEs were first disrupted by subprime lending in 2005-2007. GSE market shares fell as Wall Street encouraged lenders to snap together ways to cut the time and costs out of a mortgage loan. In response, the GSE's joined the game but not with the most responsible originators. Responding to federal "affordable market share" requirements, the GSEs bought their way into the subprime market in bulk transactions. Remember "Fast and Easy?" It quickly turned into "Fast and Sleazy."

How could this occur? Wall Street had an imperfect understanding of layered risk and an imperfect understanding of housing prices. Originators responded to this imperfect understanding by selling products with layered risk during a housing price bubble. The question was, "Can I get this loan sold?", not "Will this loan perform?" Wall Street was relying on overcollateralization and the representations and warranties of the originators.

These very originators, too, had an imperfect understanding of the contracts they executed with the GSEs and correspondents. Most contracts had no materiality or causality language regarding defects. The most egregious contracts had the correspondent purchaser as the sole arbiter of a defect and the remedies associated with that defect. Quinn Emanuel Trial Lawyers earned their moniker, a "Global Force in Business Litigation,"[35] by building a large-scale machine that successfully sued originators over a variety of alleged defects, trifling or otherwise, on behalf of their clients.

The response to the first disruption was predictable: countless former homeowners with credit blemishes, substantial regression in housing prices, "Underwater mortgages" and "Strategic Defaults," the federal government using Dodd-Frank and its newly created regulations and agencies to search for and punish the guilty and those presumed guilty. Innovation in lending stopped. Period.

Qualified Mortgage guidelines hardcoded a 43% debt to income ratio into the mortgage industry. Regulation by enforcement stifled credit availability. Litigation and reputation risk chilled virtually all innovation in depository banks.

In 2017, ninety-five percent of the mortgage loans originated were backed by the GSEs or FHA. FreddieMac's overall LTV on the 2017 book was 76% with an average credit score of 746.[36] DTI was not

---

[35] www.quinnemanuel.com

[36] http://www.freddiemac.com/investors/financials/pdf/10k_021518.pdf

reported in FreddieMac's 2017 10K.[37] The pristine credit quality of the origination vintages of 2012-2017 will be the root cause of the second disruption of the GSEs, as discussed earlier.

Mortgage Originations

Note: Enterprise & Ginnie Mae includes: Freddie Mac, Fannie Mae, and Ginnie Mae.

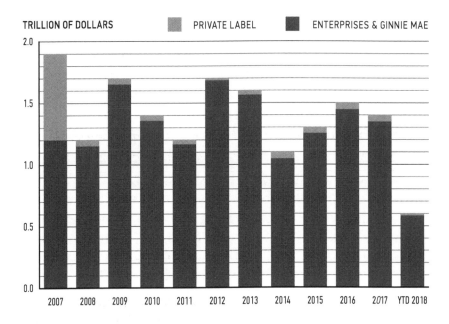

How will it manifest? The GSEs will be disrupted because their value proposition doesn't support guarantee fees of 40-45 basis points. The market is already telegraphing this—after all, jumbo to conventional mortgage spreads are negative. This means that the credit guarantee fees of the GSEs are mispriced. A cynic would say that the guarantee fees are there to pay for past sins and to feed the Treasury dividends.

---

[37] Ibid.

JAMES M. DEITCH CPA, CMB

Whatever the reason, the GSEs will be squeezed between the emerging private mortgage market and the FHA. The FHA will continue to provide low down payment loans to borrowers that fit the FHA credit box. The bread and butter GSE borrowers, 750 FICO, less than 90% LTV, will be siphoned off into the private mortgage market. Barrett Burns of VantageScore provided excellent insight into the issues of underserved borrowers and the GSE reluctance to adopt an arguably more inclusive credit scoring model[38] in my previous book, and that discussion on credit access is worth reviewing. The private mortgage market consists of bank portfolio lenders, private label securitizers, fixed income buyers, including mutual funds, sovereign wealth funds, and other investment funds.

Thinking to the future, Brent Chandler, CEO of FormFree, and I spent four hours discussing the future, particularly with respect to private mortgage lenders. Brent and I bantered, with Brent supplying the brainpower to develop the scenarios, about a world where a customer's financial DNA – every detail in a financial profile– were kept up to date in real-time and where a customer's capacity, ability, and willingness to pay could be evaluated on the fly for any type of credit.

We spoke about a customer permission-based technology that would create a customer financial record in a blockchain secure environment, obtaining permission-based feed from financial

---

[38] Barret noted that there approximately 155 million "conventional consumers" (i.e., consumers who meet a conventional scoring model's minimum criteria of having at least one account that has been opened for a period of at least six months or has account activity that has been reported in the previous six months) with credit accounts whose trended data might not be fully reported. If more trended data were available, that would impact approximately 123 million of those consumers. About 39% (or 48 million) of those consumers would see significant (20-point or more) changes in their current credit score; 20% of those consumers would see an improvement in their credit scores; and 19% would see a decline in their credit scores. Lower-scoring consumers would likely see score improvements and lenders would be able to segment higher-scoring consumers even more accurately.

institutions, investment managers, payroll data sources, credit reporting agencies, employers, the IRS, social media, and other public sources of data.

Let's walk through a more detailed scenario for the disruption to come so that you can get the full picture:

Insta-Loan: The borrower logs on to a lender's website and provides basic data – name, address, property address if purchasing . The borrower scans their driver's license and takes a selfie. The borrower authorizes e-disclosure, credit, and access to their financial data.

Behind the scenes, the following actions happen simultaneously:

- The license barcode scan is decoded and sent to the state motor vehicle department for validation. The selfie is compared to the driver's license photo via visual classification and comparison. The borrower's identity is now proven.
- Credit is pulled and the data stream is captured.
- Lien and judgment data are collected from Lexis/Nexis.
- Bank and investment account data is accessed, and twelve months data on bank account activity and investment account activity is captured as a trusted data stream.
- A collateral analysis is obtained identifying market value based upon market conditions, subject analysis, sale and listing history analysis, market sales analysis, sales data from MLS and public record sources, maps, and aerial imagery.
- Fraud screening identifies possible borrower and collateral fraud indicators.
- An electronic title review is performed.
- Disclosures are issued.
- A loan commitment is issued an AI driven AUS.

All of this happens in a matter of a few minutes. All the data is direct source data– nothing comes from the borrower. In the next instant, the data streams are evaluated against a credit risk model.

The credit score and equity in the home (that is, down payment or difference between market value and existing liens) are the primary risk measures. The credit score is a look at financial responsibility based on the borrower's behavior of meeting obligations. Equity is skin in the game.

12-month bank and investment account data streams provide a history of liquid assets and sources and uses of funds. A residual income model calculates historical cash flow to historical uses of cash, as well as liquid assets over time.

Matt Durkee of NBT Bank noted the unique position a bank has with respect to its customers:

> *"We have that data before it ever gets out to anybody else. We have the bank account and loan data for all of our consumer customers for 12 months, we have it back to account opening! We have a large amount of data on our commercial lending customers. Banks haven't figured out how to use it.*
>
> *We don't mine that data like we should. But we've got a huge advantage of knowing our customer through the banking relationship and the data generated by the banking relationship.*
>
> *Mining that data with predictive analytics can be done with first-generation data. We don't need DIC, as we already have the data and we hold many loans in portfolio. The revised QM regulations can really help banks be better competitors, especially if we couple the data and reasonable*

underwriting criteria. There's a space for bank-led 'make sense' lending that overlaps with the non-QM lending being pioneered by private label lenders."

The risk model evaluates credit score, residual income, liquid assets, and equity in the home against a scoring model. A credit decision is rendered. A private mortgage investor could commit to the loan subject only to an inspector walkthrough of the house to ensure the internal condition was commensurate with the collateral analysis.

All in, the process would take about 15 minutes, with a technology cost stack of *fewer than one hundred dollars*. The only barrier to closing the loan that same day would be TRID compliance for a first or second lien closed-end loan. The federal government has hardcoded disclosure related delays into the process.

And what about marketing costs? If a lender offered this process today and passed half the cost savings, about $4,000 to the consumer, customers would find the lender.

Consider the Conversant and Epsilon technologies discussed earlier, aimed at a servicing portfolio, coupled with Insta-Loan. One could mine the servicing portfolio for first lien, second lien, and reverse mortgage customers, not to mention for personal, auto, and student loans.

This capability exists today, and many parties, including Uber, Apple, Google, and Amazon, are thinking about how to snap technologies together to dominate the lending market.

What's holding this up? It's not the technology. Rather, it is acceptance by the GSEs, bank regulators, and capital markets. In other words, the technology exists today, but widespread acceptance of that technology *for mortgages* does not. If the applicant were applying for a credit card, personal loan, or auto loan, existing technology with a much shorter data stack can make a credit decision in a few minutes. It's as if the industry is hard-wired to respond, "It's a mortgage loan, it has to take 30 days."

Crazy. There's nothing inherently different between a mortgage loan and a credit card. Both expect that the borrower will pay as agreed. The mortgage loan has a second way out through liquidation of the collateral. That's it. But that collateral element adds layers of complexity, as does regulatory complexity.

Changes in residential lending won't happen with a big bang, but the rate of change will accelerate. One can see the edges of disruption in plain sight.

VISUAL CLASSIFICATION AND DATA EXTRACTION

Maylin Casanueva of Teraverde stated:

> *"The ability to visually classify documents and extract key data elements from these documents exists today. This technology can greatly increase the efficiency of the mortgage lending process, especially in Third Party Origination and Whole Loan Sale/Purchase transactions."*

A whole loan bulk purchase can be expedited by ingesting an unindexed PDF file of 800 pages, visually classifying the file into each document type within the file, sorting them, exercising version control over the documents to find the most current document of each type, indexing the documents, preparing a missing document list based upon the minimum necessary documents for the loan type, extracting key data from the digital images, and identifying errors or potential data integrity issues without any human "stare and compare" reviews. Best of all, the visually classified documents can be integrated into an LOS and also permanently stored for enterprise access throughout the life of the loan. This capability exists today."

One can apply this technology for delegated correspondent or wholesale transactions. The workflow and timing changes, but the building blocks to accomplish the task are constructed in a workflow that suits each channel.

One could also create a waterfall for a retail or direct-to-consumer loan that used D1C and single source validation, and at the same time ingest, classify, and extract data from documents provided by the borrower. Any misses on D1C or single source could be supplemented by the borrower supplied documents. The waterfall could use the highest quality data provided and discard unneeded data. In a few minutes, a lender would know how much data was delivered by a single source, how much was supplemented, and have a listing of missing critical documents pushed to a mobile device or email account. A conditional approval would also be provided.

BLOCKCHAIN

Henry Santos, responsible for the mortgage financial services vertical at IBM, kindly invited me to a session at IBM's Thomas J. Watson Research Center to delve into blockchain with a small group of financial executives.

What does blockchain do? According to IBM, blockchain is a shared unchangeable ledger for recording the history of transactions. In mortgage banking, these transactions could include the receipt of trusted borrower information, such as bank account data, income data, and related qualifying information. The data comes from a trusted source, such as a bank, the IRS, or payroll service, and never needs to be re-verified.

For example, the bank account records, say 12 months of transaction data, can be provided by a bank to a mortgage blockchain regarding a borrower. Same for payroll data; *data*, not images. The same goes for credit report data. One now has *trusted source* data regarding a borrower that is immutable and can be utilized by authorized parties. Same for mortgage payment history, prior credit events, collateral information, etc. This authenticated history is permissioned, meaning a consumer could grant permission to a lender to access this trusted information.

The consumer's record could also be *appended in real-time.* This means that once the basic information is created, the ongoing transactional history could be built. Imagine having an authenticated complete history of a consumer's finances available for an instant credit decision since all of the information is assembled from trusted parties! No redundant QC. No robotics. Just authentic, real-time data.

Access to this information could be granted by the customer to servicers, prospective originators, owners of the underlying loan, etc. This means the party owning the servicing could essentially offer a refinance, or additional credit or wealth management services if the consumer grants permission. The servicing asset takes on a whole new dimension as an element of the financial value chain in mortgage lending. It's not just a stream of cash flows, it's access to everything financial about the customer.

Henry Santos envisions a blockchain-powered utility that essentially collates and distributes trusted source digital information without copying it. Such technologies enable the servicing asset to be monetized in many ways. The entire history of the customer's mortgage(s) and related information could be easily utilized. Imagine having a complete digital record of the customer's application data, with all servicing and payment transaction available to the servicer. What if the customer "opted in" to let the servicer obtain a digital stream of bank transactions and payroll data? One could then literally do a refinance at the touch of a mouse or obtain a new mortgage needing only an appraisal. Or, maybe no appraisal is even needed at all.

BUILDING IN QUALITY

Brian Fitzpatrick, CEO of LoanLogics, comments on building in loan quality as opposed to fixing the data after the fact:

> *"Exacerbating the issue of loan quality are "after the fact quality control checks." This involves another set of underwriters known as "auditors" who are checking that the underwriting has been done correctly and in compliance with investor guidelines, rules and regulations. When this is performed after the loan is underwritten, but prior to closing, correcting the mistakes and errors found often requires the loan officer or processor to go back to the borrower for "just one more thing."*

> *Borrowers don't understand this and frankly don't care. They want to provide everything that is needed up-front, one time and then be left alone until closing. Almost every borrower has complained about this back-and-forth process.*

JAMES M. DEITCH CPA, CMB

Then, 'quality control' happens again after the loan closes, but prior to shipping to an investor, creating another chance where the lender might need to go back to the borrower. And, the possibility exists for more errors to be found as a loan is delivered to the investor and they perform their pre-purchase due diligence of the file. All this can lead to a series of frustrating conversations with the borrower whose loan is already closed.

The crux of the problem is that loan quality checks begin too late – often after the loan has been underwritten or closed. In other words, during points at which these checks will be the most frustrating for the borrower, creating further delays, difficult conversations and/or costly lender penalties.

So why not build loans correctly from the start and check quality real time as you go?

This, essentially, is what regtech does. Regtech defines technologies that help organizations comply with regulations and all investors' lending guidelines more efficiently while reducing human labor. Using rules-driven technology, regtech can quickly analyze large amounts of data to automatically decision the loan, determine compliance and at the same time evaluate the potential risk of fraud.

DAY 1 CERTAINTY

Fannie Mae is currently piloting its Single Source Validation, a service which allows lenders to validate a borrower's income, assets, and employment through one report, using source data rather than multiple paper documents.

Single Source and services like it will likely be a big part of the future. The difficulty and challenges facing both customers and lenders are that the success rate for seeking income information through Day 1 Certainty, according to my informal discussions with lenders, is 15% or less. If a private lender is willing to compute residual income based upon the discussion above on Insta-Loan, traditional income documentation from W-2, IRS, and payroll services becomes less of a factor.

Day 1 Certainty and Single Source and similar efforts are very large steps forward and they will ultimately improve transparency and speed in mortgage lending.

ENCOMPASS LOS

During our brainstorming, Brent Chandler and I walked through LOS technology. We both agreed that Ellie Mae Encompass was a disruptive technology. Not because Encompass is an LOS, but because of the end-to-end nature of the Ellie Mae solution. While detractors may snark about the time Ellie Mae needs to roll out NextGen and a full API suite, the reality is that Encompass is disrupting competitors far and wide.

Ellie Mae pioneered 'success-based pricing,' meaning you pay a reasonable install fee, and then pay monthly based on actual closed loans. This in itself was disruptive and gained Ellie Mae considerable market share because Ellie Mae variablized the technology cost of the LOS. When competitors were competing with traditional pricing mechanisms, Ellie Mae signed up hundreds of clients large and small.

The re-roll of Encompass Consumer Connect has been impressive. The disruptive strategy was to make Consumer Connect part of the core LOS system. No additional cost and modest additional configuration. One client suggested to me that Consumer Connect has 75% of the usable functionality of third-party front-ends like Blend, Roostify, and BeSmartee at 0% of the price of the third-party frontend. That's disruptive!

Ellie Mae's roadmap (set out below) includes a healthy dose of connectivity via API, as well as an Encompass Data Connect product to access all fields, standard, custom, and virtual, quickly. One critic complained that "Ellie Mae is selling me my own data." That's one way to look at it. Look at the Ellie Mae product roadmap. It's end-to-end as a platform to connect other services and platforms. It permits snap-together solutions to be rolled out quickly. At its core is a system of record with all compliance needs built in.

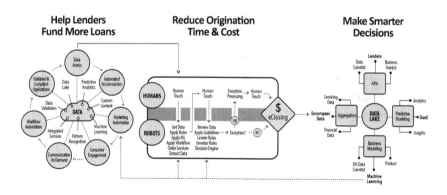

Jonathan Corr recognizes the value of data. Ellie Mae is exploiting this data with Ellie Mae Origination Insights and its Millennial Tracker reporting, all using aggregated data from Encompass users.

Another way of thinking about it is that Ellie Mae is providing a way to democratize data within a lender. Data Connect, when coupled with servicing, accounting, and other data, provides the ability to measure performance at the loan level, employee level, activity level – virtually complete granularity when coupled with the appropriate associative data engine and the broad mortgage banking domain knowledge to utilize all of the data in a lucid and useful solution.

Jonathan Corr stated, "Ellie Mae is introducing the core platform to harness disruptive technologies of Ellie Mae and related partners. There's nothing else like it in the mortgage banking industry."

The remainder of this book describes how the intersection of the levers of strategy and data-driven decision making can empower lenders to change their own game and disrupt the industry. In all this, one thing is clear– disruption is well underway across the mortgage industry. It behooves us to recognize it and learn how to harness it before it gets the best of us.

CHAPTER 4
SIX LEVERS OF STRATEGIC INTENTION

My Six Levers of Strategic Intention had their origin early in my career.

The day started as most Fridays did— wrapping up a site visit as an auditor for Arthur Andersen & Co. CPAs and getting ready to fly back home to Philadelphia in the afternoon. Arriving at the Columbus, Ohio airport, I boarded an Allegheny Airlines BAC-111 for a flight to Philadelphia as it began to rain. We taxied out and waited for 90 minutes as thunderstorms dumped rain and flashed lightning all around us. We took off, and the flight went downhill fast. Twenty minutes into the flight, the pilot came on the public address, "Flight attendants will remain seated as we have really rough weather all around us."

Forty-five minutes into the flight we headed north towards Cleveland. Then, after two hours in the air, south back towards Columbus. The pilot then announced, "It's looking pretty grim up here...we are now at minimum fuel and will land at Pittsburgh." It seems the 90-minute ground hold and two hours in the air had used up a lot of fuel.

After *three* missed approaches in Pittsburgh, the pilot announced that the flight attendants would need to describe the "brace position" to us, as we were landing on the next approach no matter what thanks to the low fuel. We landed hard, rolled out and then absolute quiet. No engine noise, no roar, just the wind and rain pelting the aircraft. We were towed into the gate by a tug, completely depleted of fuel. You could say I was, too. I abandoned the flight, rented a car, and drove back to Philadelphia, completely unwilling to get on another plane for the time being.

My fear of flying was pretty sizable for a while there. I learned to fly myself in order to overcome that fear. Early on in my lessons, Mike Sullivan, my instructor, described the four factors that affected flight: *lift, drag, weight, and thrust.* He called the factors the four levers of aerodynamics. Varying any or all of these levers controlled everything about an aircraft in flight. Flight training demonstrated how to manipulate the controls of an aircraft through all phases of flight, all the while affecting the four aerodynamic levers of lift, drag, weight, and thrust. Understanding this allowed me to overcome the fear of flying that started back on that Friday long ago.

Similarly, there are controls, or levers, of strategy. I previously described the six broad strategic levers to achieve a lender's goals in Chapter 1:

1. A lender can expand to achieve economies of scale;

2. A lender can adjust its channels of distribution;

3. A lender can become technologically and process transformative;

JAMES M. DEITCH CPA, CMB

4. A lender can exploit product niche or niches;

5. A lender can diversify beyond mortgage banking;

6. And, a lender can increase the level of relationship and empathy when interacting with prospects and customers.

The point of this anecdote is this— understanding the levers in a system gives you clarity, no matter what comes your way. Know the levers, how they affect the overall system, and how to operate them well. Similar to flying an aircraft, these levers must be carefully and smoothly moved. They are key to the high-level Strategic Transformation that the mortgage industry needs.

STRATEGIC MODEL FOR RESIDENTIAL FINANCE

One can also look at the history of a company's strategy, its current strategy, and future strategies. One can plot strategy and time on a graphic and consider a company's options, competitors' strategies, and opportunities to modify strategy going forward. The strategy map might look like this:

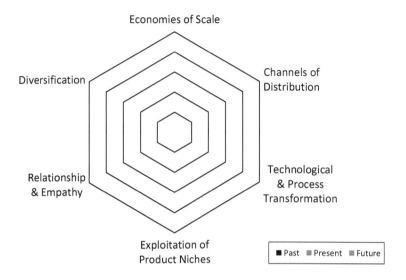

Economies of Scale

Channels of Distribution

Technological & Process Transformation

Exploitation of Product Niches

Relationship & Empathy

Diversification

■ Past ▨ Present ▨ Future

I recently had a casual conversation with a CEO. He described his strategy, which I've summarized below:

> *"We offer retail, wholesale, and correspondent channels. We have picked up several branches to build volume. Our loan officers require us to offer all product options, conventional, govvie, rural, bond money, non-QM, jumbo, you name it. Our LOS is well known, and we've adapted it for all of our channels. Our marketing and service are exceptional. We have great relationships with customers and employees. We broker commercial loans to diversify into other products. I'm actively seeking opportunities to pick up weak players."*

Here's my perception of his current strategy map. Notice that all levers of strategy are being pulled. No overarching strategy focus. One of my associates described this strategy map as 'all things to all people.'

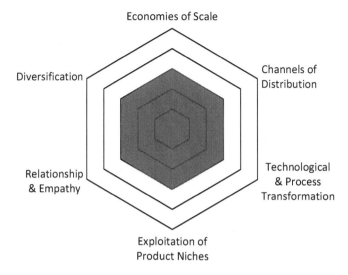

Economies of Scale

Diversification

Channels of
Distribution

Relationship
& Empathy

Technological
& Process
Transformation

Exploitation of
Product Niches

Notice that the map is covered. There's little focus on any particular lever or focus on all levers. My perception is that an 'all things to all people' strategy won't work. In fact, it's no strategy at all. Let's contrast that to the strategies used by Quicken in the past, present, and future[39].

Bill Emerson, Vice-Chair of Rock Holding Inc, and former CEO of Quicken described early strategy at the company. Initially, Quicken was a traditional lender focusing on growing the retail branch business, the economies of scale, while exploring online lending.

> *"I started with Rock Financial In 1993. We were a branch originator. And by the time 1998 rolled around, we had about 30 branches around the country. And there was an*

---

[39] Please note that the discussion of strategy levers is my independent analysis based upon research and discussion with Quicken employees and others in the industry. My discussion of strategy levels should not suggest that my independent analysis of Quicken is endorsed by any employee of Quicken or is an authorized description of Quicken's internal strategies. My effort here is to define a process to map strategy, and the discussion of Quicken is illustrative only.

e-mail that Dan [Gilbert] sent internally to a group of people in 1998 that basically said we are behind the eight ball. The internet is the way to go.

He had read an article about a company that was trying to do some stuff on the Internet and that we needed to, you know, get on it and start figuring out this business model or we'd get left behind. Now, this is 1998. So, when we started out we took about six, seven smart people, put them in a room, and started building a website. And that website was called Rockloan.com. And actually, that was a website, that back in 1999, you could literally have credit pulled, you could lock in interest rate if you wanted to."

The strategic map of this early strategy follows:

QUICKEN EARLY STRATEGY (LATE 1990'S)

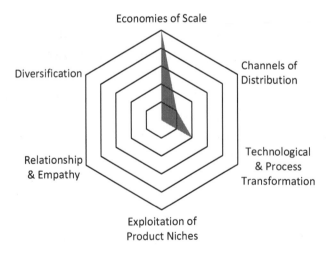

Notice there is a focus, building the retail channel using some elements of technology. Bill mentioned that the focus on technology and direct lending became laser-focused. Bill shared an anecdote about Quicken's transition to a proprietary technology-based direct lender.

> "Dan [Gilbert] was wandering by the room where the group had built the website and asked what was going on. He asked, 'How many people were visiting the site?' Somebody said, 'We had about 50 visits.' Dan said, '50 visits! We're shutting down all the branches and we're going to the internet only.' Then somebody goes, 'Wait wait, Dan. forty-seven of the fifty were just testing the website. Dan said, 'I don't care. We are getting out of the branch model and going to the internet only.'
>
> The reality of it is something along those lines, but we really did say we've got to start focusing on a centralized model and we did decide to go out and shut down every branch outside of the state of Michigan."

That strategy evolved to allow Quicken to be a direct, online lender and focus on developing technology and processes in order to excel at customer service. Quicken gave up on their prior retail strategy and focused solely on direct-to-consumer lending. This focus propelled Quicken to impressive growth, allowing the company to achieve economies of scale, as well as outstanding customer service. While Quicken is privately held, it is well understood that Quicken also attains superior profitability.

Quicken's current strategy is presented below. Notice how the elements of strategy levers key to Quicken jump out. Economies of scale focus on a singular channel, not four or five channels, and a heavy focus on technology and process transformation.

QUICKEN STRATEGY (PRESENT)

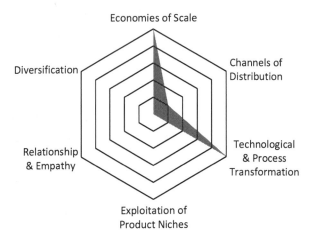

Bill describes the benefit of this sharp focus:

"You blend in technology and the ability for people to communicate with you any way they want…except face to face. It really makes their lives much simpler, much easier. There's a certain aspect of being able to do what you do and be able to conduct a pretty complicated financial transaction from your kitchen table if you want to. And if done well and done correctly, with the right technology, with the right visibility, and with the right philosophy around client service then you can win seven years in a row for J.D. Power on the origination side, in four years or so for J.D. Power on the servicing side. [The years we won number one] were the only years we've been eligible because there's a certain amount of sample size you've got to have in order to be able to be there and to win."

Clayton Christensen, the author of "Innovator's Dilemma" who may have first identified disruption, might have been thinking of Quicken when he stated, "When a company identifies how to integrate the processes needed to give the consumer a sense of job completion, it can blow away the competition. A product is easy to copy, but experiences are very hard to replicate."

Quicken achieved the number one rating in origination and servicing by focusing on the direct-to-consumer retail strategy, powered by technology that contemplates that a Quicken employee will never meet a customer face to face. That is the power of commitment and focus to the key levers of strategy. And that commitment to the technology lever continued with the launch of Rocket Mortgage, according to Bill Emerson:

> "It's been interesting to watch the industry struggle to embrace technology. I think we probably started a little bit of an avalanche with RocketMortgage and made people realize that they needed to step into the game and so you're starting to see more and more of that [technological investment] happen."

And those levers of strategy complement Quicken's culture and belief system:

> "I can't emphasize enough how important culture is, and the mindset and belief system of 'every client, every time, no exceptions, no excuses.' Does the number one position for J.D. Power origination and servicing come out of the culture or is that culture driven by that desire to be number one? [We have 19 sayings, or "Quickenisms", that convey our culture and strategy]: it's not just simply 19 sayings written on a piece of paper. There is an entire methodology around that."

Quicken is now moving to expand niche products beyond conventional, FHA, VA, and jumbo. That additional focus on niche products can be seen on the strategy map below.

QUICKEN STRATEGY (FUTURE)

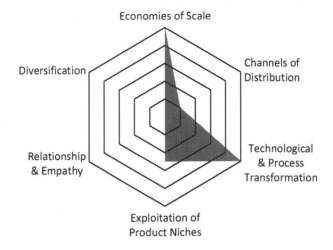

I marvel at how consistent Quicken's strategy map has been, focusing on three levers over 20 years, and achieving outstanding results.

QUICKEN STRATEGY

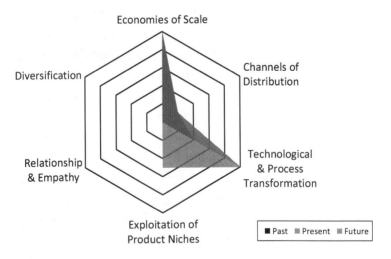

Let's examine the strategies of other lenders using this same strategic model. Note that the definition of a particular company's strategy is the author's opinion, and has not been verified or endorsed by the respective companies. The illustrative nature of these descriptions is to further the understanding of the strategic model map, not peg a particular set of strategies to a particular lender.

JP MORGAN CHASE

JP Morgan Chase has a 200-year history, assets over $2.5 trillion, and a presence in over 100 markets globally. Historically, the institution's mortgage strategy included economies of scale and multiple channels of distribution largely through GSE, FHA, and Private Label channels. The financial crisis saw the bank withdraw from Private Label and FHA lending and substantially reduce its third-party origination channels.

But now, Chase is embarking on multiple changes across its strategic levers. In a recent overview, Chase reported that it is embarking on "digital everything," including Finn – a mobile-only banking platform and Chase Auto Direct digital car buying service powered by TrueCar that allows customers to pick a car and secure financing in one place.

In mortgages, the Roostify partnership is said to transform the Chase Digital Mortgage process into a simpler, faster, and more transparent process. This new process accounts for about a 15% reduction in time to complete the mortgage refinance process.[40] Chase views jumbo product now as a balance sheet asset as opposed to a securitization asset, as well as a method to secure and retain wealth management customers.

[40] JPMorgan Chase Strategic Update, Marianne Lake, Chief Financial Officer, February 27, 2018.

JP MORGAN CHASE STRATEGY

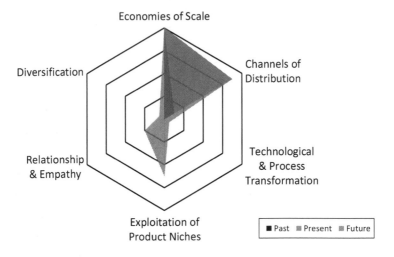

FREEDOM MORTGAGE

Freedom Mortgage was a large GSE lender, pursuing scale in the lead-up to the financial crisis. When liquidity began to ebb from the capital markets in 2007, Stan Middleman, Freedom's founder and CEO pivoted quickly to FHA and VA lending. One can see the strategic levers being adjusted by Mr. Middleman:

> *When you are a small company, you have small issues. Big companies, big issues. [During 2007 and 2008, large companies] needed a lot of liquidity to get by. It was a real problem. So [for Freedom] it was really a liquidity issue at the end of the day. We took a route that created the safest loans possible. We were 90 percent GSE going into 2007. By 2008, we were 90 percent Ginnie Mae. Ginnie Mae provided liquidity by statute. Statutory liquidity is*

far different than discretionary liquidity. [By the end of 2008], we were in a pretty good place because we made that strategic change to focus on Ginnie Mae lending.

In the ensuing period, Freedom expanded its third-party channels and began offering more niche products. One of its niches is a servicing product. Freedom offers its Eagle Eye Pledge, providing oversight of a borrowers' loan by finding lower rates during the time the loan is serviced by Freedom, or by helping a borrower extract cash from increasing home equity in a home, or when Freedom has a product or service that may benefit a borrower. This pledge appears to be an early adoption of a 'customer for life' strategy, consistent with Stan Middleman's view that servicing is a strategic asset. Freedom was an early investor in Matic. Matic Insurance Services, a digital homeowners insurance agency that allows mortgage borrowers to buy homeowners insurance during the mortgage transaction or during the servicing life of a loan.

FREEDOM MORTGAGE STRATEGY

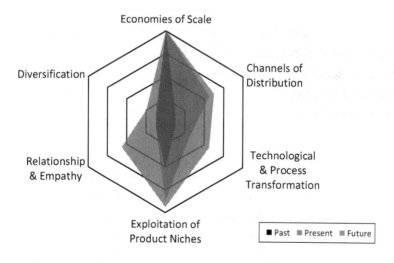

ANGEL OAK COMPANIES

Angel Oak Companies specialize in non-QM and niche products, along with a fully integrated vertical structure from retail and TPO origination, through securitization and mutual fund investors. As Steven Schwalb, CEO and Managing Partner of Angel Oak Home Loans said, "We're constantly finding innovative ways to develop outside the box products that are valuable to our clients."

In a discussion with Mr. Schwalb, this innovative spirit emerges with loan products aimed at the non-QM space. "Done properly, these loans perform well and are in the consumer's interest." This continual focus on vertical integration, an economies of scale strategy, and product niches provides a consistent strategy for growth and market acceptance. Mr. Schwalb states that consistency pays off: "Three years ago, few people returned our calls. Now everyone is calling us because we are the largest PLS (private label securitizer) in the market."

Angel Oak employs a heavy dose of the Product Niche strategic lever, coupled with Channels of Distribution and a Relationship Focus. According to Steven Schwalb:

> "We started with a large retail origination focus, which adds the relationship focus. The retail channel has evolved to distributing products best suited to face-to-face relationship building. I'm a big believer that every family should have a great life with a place to call home. I believe if people can demonstrate that, they can handle a loan as long as it's reasonable and doesn't expose the family to unexpected risk.
>
> Can you imagine being a parent and you had a foreclosure because you had to get a job in another city? And you're

upside down in the house. You have to tell your wife and children to not get sick because we have no savings. It's very hard for me to say to that family you don't deserve another house, ever.

I think customers who have demonstrated responsibility after the crisis are the ones we want to lend to.

These parents should be able to look at their children in the eyes and say, 'Go paint your bedroom pink. Go with stars or horses or ponies on the walls.' Our borrowers don't have to worry about their rate going up next year. But in my core, I'm thinking about all the families who have been in difficulty that need help to buy a home.

As our products took hold, we started to distribute through wholesale brokers and then correspondents. Not every customer fits into a GSE loan, and we serve that space."

ANGEL OAK STRATEGY

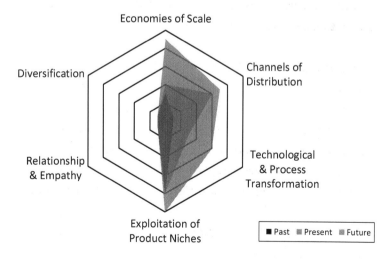

CASCADE FINANCIAL SERVICES

Cascade focuses on manufactured housing, following a Product Niche strategy. According to Cody Pearce of Cascade:

> *"We provide a product that some in the industry don't believe in. I believe in it. Firmly. I am a huge fan of manufactured housing. I have been since we started doing this and I began educating myself on it. I believe it is one of the key solutions to the affordable housing deficit that we have in the United States. I think manufactured housing is currently and will continue to play a significant role in filling the affordable housing void.*

To correctly underwrite loans and loan performance, we've had to mine all of that data out of previous portfolios and work with industry partners to acquire and accumulate as much real-time data as possible.

Cascade has an advantage in that some manufactured housing units are treated as real estate loans when the housing unit is permanently affixed to a foundation. Manufactured housing units that are not permanently affixed are treated as chattel loans, i.e., a loan secured by non-real estate collateral.

> *"The private label market is developing for manufactured housing loans, especially since Berkshire-Hathaway has multiple investments in manufactured housing producers, and a captive mortgage company serving buyers. Warren Buffet is viewed as 'very smart money,' and the Berkshire-led manufacturers are producing high-quality housing at affordable price points."*

CASCADE STRATEGY

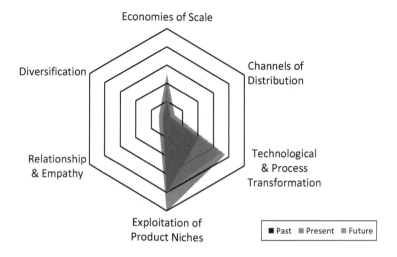

Economies of Scale

Diversification

Channels of
Distribution

Relationship
& Empathy

Technological
& Process
Transformation

Exploitation of
Product Niches

■ Past ▨ Present ▨ Future

The purpose of profiling banks and mortgage bankers is not to suggest a particular strategy. Rather, the profiles demonstrate how to apply a strategic map to any lender's business. The strategy over time dimension helps one evaluate how strategy has been deployed over time, and how historical strategy links to future strategy.

DEVELOPING YOUR OWN STRATEGIC LEVERS

As a wrap up to this chapter, let's take a look at how you can develop your own strategic levers at your company. To begin, consider a past/present/future strategic map of your business. Feel free to fill out the following blank map:

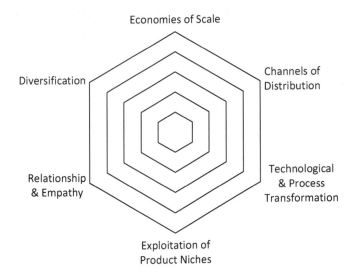

Please consider your business model and how you would disrupt it if you were a competitor. Ask yourself:

What would you do to really hit your business in its soft spots?

Then consider how you might move the following strategic levers to defend your business:

1. Is it favorable for your business to expand to achieve economies of scale? Expansion for economies of scale can include hiring sales personnel, like Loan Officers or Account Executives, and adding geography to serve. How would/could you achieve economies of scale?

2. Is it favorable for your business to adjust its channels of distribution? This includes adding channels such as direct-to-consumer, traditional retail, wholesale, correspondent, bulk

purchase, bundling distribution of product with another service, and realtor or builder joint ventures.

3. Is it favorable for your business to become technologically and process transformative? Would process automation, additional technology to augment core applications such as LOS, etc., be appropriate? Would you consider becoming a first mover into transformative technologies such as blockchain, AI, etc.?

4. Is it favorable for your business to exploit product niche or niches? Product niches can include non-QM, rehab, construction-to-perm, fix and flip, investment property, alternate income qualification methods, etc.

5. Is it favorable for your business to diversify beyond consumer mortgage banking? This includes consumer lending, insurance, commercial real estate lending, wealth management, etc.

6. Is it favorable for your business to creatively and systemically focus on relationship building and empathy when interacting with customers?

These questions are a great place for you and your team to start. Sit with these ideas and explore how they define your company. Later on in this book, we'll revisit these questions with a little more detail on how to implement your chosen lever(s).

CHAPTER 5

DATA-DRIVEN ENTERPRISES

A colleague and I sat down one evening in Buckhead, Atlanta for an early dinner. I had been at the restaurant twice previously. The server, Joseph, walked up and said, "Jim, great to see you back. How about you start your evening with a Sazerac?" I was a bit surprised. My colleague ordered some wine, and I bit on the Sazerac offer. How did he know I liked Sazeracs?

Drinks delivered, Joseph then suggested either a charcuterie platter or a cheese platter as a starter while we reviewed the menu. At this point, I knew some form of customer relationship/retention platform was in use— Joseph knew that's what I had last time.

He was startled when I asked point blank, "Why are you using data from my last visit here?" He then smiled and said it helped get customers comfortable and make them feel that their preferences were noticed by the restaurant. "There are a lot of good restaurants in Atlanta, and we have to stand out," said Joseph.

It turns out Joseph worked at the restaurant part-time as a server. His day job was an administrator for a company that used SalesForce, the customer relationship management software, as a service tool. He was very proud to use data from the restaurant's CRM, because "most people don't use it, and it helps me provide good service and earn a good tip."

The restaurant example is perhaps an easier example of data-driven customer service. What it really illustrates, however, is that data is one of the most transformative factors in any business today, in any industry. The way we parse and engage with data in mortgage banking, in particular, can give us what we need to utilize our Six Strategic Levers most effectively.

DATA DRIVEN BASEBALL

The Oakland Athletics, or the "A's" as some fans call them, have a long and storied history. The A's appeared in three consecutive World Series, from 1988 through 1990, and had the highest payroll in baseball in 1991. New owners Stephen Schott and Ken Hofmann slashed payroll. As a result, Billy Beane had to work on a strategy to obtain relatively undervalued players. He valued on-base percentage among hitters. This strategy flew in the face of conventional major league baseball scouting methods.

Beane crafted a cost-efficient but winning team. By the 2006 MLB season, the Athletics ranked 24th out of 30 major league teams in player salaries but had the 5th-best regular-season record. The Oakland A's became the first team in the 100 plus years of American League baseball to win 20 consecutive games. They won their first playoff series under Beane in 2006 when they swept the Minnesota Twins in the American League Division Series. *All on a modest payroll.*

Beane's strategy worked because baseball teams had accumulated a vast amount of data on every player's at-bat performance, fielding performance, tendencies, etc. This data, however, was not used by teams in the same way as Beane used it. The analytics done for Beane provided insight into what performance factors into games ('on base percentage'), and one could obtain players that were not viewed as 'stars' but had good 'on base' production while being paid modestly.

Remember, it's all about the runs. And to earn runs, you have to get on base.

The strategy is still working, as the Oakland A's have the lowest aggregate salary cost as of opening day 2018. Here is the salary listing[41]:

2018 MLB OPENING DAY PAYROLLS

RANK	TEAM	PAYROLL ($ MILLIONS)	RANK	TEAM	PAYROLL ($ MILLIONS)
1	Boston Red Sox	235.7	16	Cleveland Indians	134.4
2	San Francisco Giants	208.5	17	Arizona Diamondbacks	132.5
3	Los Angeles Dodgers	186.1	18	Minnesota Twins	131.9
4	Chicago Cubs	183.5	19	Detriot Tigers	129.9
5	Washington Nationals	181.6	20	Kansas City Royals	129.9
6	Los Angeles Angels	175.1	21	Altanta Braves	120.5
7	New York Yankees	168.5	22	Cincinnati Reds	101.2
8	Seattle Mariners	162.5	23	Miami Marlins	98.6
9	Toronto Blue Jays	162.3	24	Philadelphia Phillies	96.9
10	St. Louis Cardinals	161.0	25	San Diego Padres	96.1
11	Houston Astros	160.0	26	Miwaukee Brewers	90.2
12	New York Mets	154.6	27	Pittsburgh Pirates	87.9
13	Texas Rangers	144.0	28	Tampa Bay Rays	78.7
14	Baltimore Orioles	143.1	29	Chicago White Sox	72.2
15	Colorado Rockies	141.3	30	Oakland Athletics	68.5

[41] http://www.stevetheump.com/Payrolls.htm

Following are the 2018 American League West, the division where the Oakland A's play, standings as of August 20, 2018, and the cost per win:

2018 AL WEST AUGUST 20, 2018	WON	LOST	ANNUAL PAYROLL	COST PER WIN ($ MILLIONS)
Houston	75	49	160.0	1.65
Oakland	74	50	68.5	0.71
Seattle	71	54	162.5	1.77
L.A. Angels	63	63	175.1	2.14
Texas	56	70	144.0	1.15

Source: MLB

The Oakland A's currently have the lowest cost per win, at $710,000 by far. The A's strategy is not only to use data-driven analytics to get the best players at the lowest cost but to also use data-driven analysis to coach the player to maximize getting on base— the precursor to runs which are the precursor to wins.

When A's players are about to go free-agent and become eligible for large contracts, the A's either trade them away or just refuse to offer them an expensive contracts. They replace departing players with new, often minor, players who are still inexpensive.

It's a more than a workable strategy. But, more importantly, it's a strategy that is durable. It's worked for the A's over time. The A's win games at a fraction of the high-salary teams. At the end of the day in baseball, it's about cost per win.

	2001				2018			
	WINS	SALARY ($ MILLIONS)	COST PER WIN ($ MILLIONS)	RELATIVE COST PER WIN TO MOST EXPENSIVE TEAM	WINS	SALARY ($ MILLIONS)	COST PER WIN (IN MILLIONS)	RELATIVE COST PER WIN TO MOST EXPENSIVE TEAM
NY Yankees	95	109.8	$1.16	100%	78	208.5	$2.06	100%
Boston	82	109.6	$1.34	116%	88	235.7	$2.07	100%
Oakland	102	33.8	$0.33	29%	75	68.5	$0.71	34%

Source: MLB

One would think that mortgage bankers would focus on minimizing the cost per loan and/or maximizing the profit per loan. When I ask a mortgage banker about their business statistics, the first quantitative description that they mention is the dollar volume of originations. A natural answer, since that scopes out the basic scale of the operation. But volume is not a description of the lender's profitability, health, cash flow, or long-term viability.

It's not an industry secret—many mortgage bankers are enthralled by volume. Entry into the top 100 or top 10 lenders is an aspirational goal for many, and it has set the standard of success for decades. Is this devotion to volume over profit beneficial to the mortgage banking industry in the long run?

Some lenders view volume as a metric of success. "We have 7 of the top 100 loan officers in the country." This is a metric based on volume, but are these loan officers profitable? When I ask a CEO about company profit, the answer is usually, "We're better than peer." Statistically, half the time this may be true. The other half of the time, it is not. Not everyone can be "better than peer." C level executives of lenders don't seem to focus on profit as much as other industries, according to Martin Kerr of Loan Vision. The exception is publicly traded lenders, where profitability is transparent due to public reporting requirements.

Why the focus on volume when it is clear that size does not matter in mortgage banking? The chart that follows depicts pre-tax profit by lender size, expressed as basis points of loan volume. The data suggests lenders of almost any size can be profitable. It also suggests that the strategy—originator compensation structure, loan product, channel, and operational construct—is more predictive of profit than just volume. The largest lenders had the highest profit in only one of the five years. Large volume does not necessarily mean large profit.

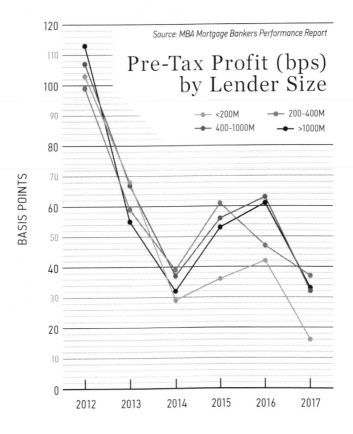

Needless to say, lunch with Billy Beane provided a lot of food for thought. We briefly touched on how one might apply Moneyball thinking to mortgage banking, but I've continued to think about it in the ensuing years. Mortgage banking is just as rich in statistics as baseball—and ready for this kind of creative disruption.

BASEBALL STATS MEET MORTGAGE BANKING—MORTGAGE BALL

The Oakland A's focused on the cost per win and coached their low-cost players on how to get on base, as mentioned, the true precursor to winning a game. In other words, very specific coaching at a particular set of strategic baseball levers. One lever is a team-wide approach to batting strategy.

Baseball players like to hit the ball. It's the moment that defines the game for many, and crowd-pleasing home runs and well-struck baseballs always bring the crowd to their feet. But letting each batter hit as they wish forgoes two strategic levers.

The first lever involving opposing pitcher strategy is pretty straightforward— Take a lot of pitches and force the starting pitcher out early.

A snippet of a coaching scene in the movie "Moneyball" illustrates this concept: Mark Ellis played second base for the A's. Billy Beane tells Ellis: "You want to see more pitches and get deep into their bullpen. You want to get your at-bats off their 10th or 11th [relief] pitcher." Ellis says incredulously, "You want us to walk more?" Peter Brand replies, "At least once in every ten at-bats." Ellis likes to hit, so he says, "Or..." Beane replies, "Triple-A Sacramento is only 80 miles away," meaning if Ellis doesn't follow directions, he'll be demoted to the minor leagues. In order to implement a high-level strategic approach, Beane has to ask baseball players to work against what they've always thought about the game.

The second strategic lever is getting on base more by analyzing each batter's performance, or when the batter attempts to hit the ball.

Ray Durham also played second base for the A's. Peter Brand shows Durham a chart of data-driven analytics regarding Durham's batting averages depending on when he swings at a pitch. "Basically, these are all your at-bats. This is you versus righties, you versus lefties... and then, of course, all your count knowledge, okay? In an 0-0 count [meaning the first pitch is coming now], you're batting .290. In an 0-1 [first pitch was a strike] you average .238. In an 0-2, .159. When you're 1-0 [the first pitch was a ball], you're batting .324. Understand what I'm saying?"

Durham's response is telling. "But I'm a first-pitch hitter. I like to swing at fastballs." Brand tells him, "And that's the way you've been trained. But it's a habit we'd like to break you from. We're trying to design the game to your strengths. This has nothing to do with you being a great hitter— you're a great hitter. We just want to get you on base."

Beane tells the players, "I'm interested in you getting on base. If you do that, we win. If you don't, we lose."

Beane told me that the movie is pretty accurate with regards to his strategy, though Beane said that he is more personable and better looking than Brad Pitt, who played him in Moneyball. "Find out the key metric in any business, and design strategy around that key metric. In baseball, the key metric is getting on base."

Imagine coaching a production team with this degree of data.

"MORTGAGE BALL"

Maylin Casanueva of Teraverde performed analytics by comparing the all in revenue generated by a loan officer compared to the 'all in' compensation costs of the loan officer to compute profit contribution margin. The results were surprising, in that the highest volume loan officers were rarely the most profitable. What if we created a method that I'll call Mortgage Ball? (with thanks to Billy Beane for coining the term during our discussion at the MBA lunch) The Mortgage Ball method would seek out loan officers that closed loans for the highest contribution profit margin per loan, and lowest cost to originate. Ms. Casanueva stated:

"Data driven analytical techniques work in baseball and in mortgage banking. Just like the Oakland A's, there are originators who are very profitable because they produce loans with higher margins (such as FHA loans), require few cures, are properly structured and move through the system quickly, and the LO compensation is constructed to maximize company. The key to profitability for a lender is to establish a 'cut line' for loan contribution margin in dollars and in basis points. Fall below the cut line (or fail to get above it) for more than 60 days, and lender profit suffers. Do lenders know their own 'cut line?' If not, it's difficult to manage profitability.

And just like the A's, lenders can profile the type of loan officer that produces the most contribution margin and recruit those loan officers. And for the less or non-profitable loan officers, do yourself a favor and cut them.

This process works equally well for the TPO channels. Find the brokers or correspondents that provide the most profit, after cures and fallout, establish a cut line, and follow it."

Getting into more detail, we could rank loan officers from highest to lowest contribution margin, based on the profitability of the product mix, since Dodd-Frank prevents compensation on loan terms, such as different commissions for FHA versus conventional, and the aggregate commissions, salary and bonus costs for each loan officer. We will use an anonymized dataset to look at actual results, with anonymized loan officers, etc. We would do the same for branches. Think of the branches as teams in a league.

Here are the standings of one lender, showing the top eight and bottom five loan officers out of 200 plus originators for two quarters. Notice that volume is nowhere on this chart. Units, total revenue, total compensation, and contribution margin tell the story. We'll get into the details later in the book, but study this chart. If you were recruiting from this lender, who would you want on your team?

Contribution Margin Analysis

LOAN OFFICER	UNITS	TOTAL REVENUE ($)	TOTAL COMP. ($)	TOTAL CONTRIB. MARGIN ($)
Imelda Madelyn Key	93	1,359,491	263,110	1,096,382
Jeffrey Hart	87	1,059,349	230,000	829,349
Lucille Simon	96	1,205,799	437,500	768,299
Wilfredo Robby Klein	75	921,310	223,000	698,310
Lewis Chaney	104	807,466	145,814	661,651
Theron Vargas	55	728,117	101,546	626,571
Ivy Weber	46	624,237	124,100	500,137
Tyson Kline	58	640,327	164,994	475,333
Leonel Prince	59	644,703	184,010	460,693
Ty Johnnie Cotton	2	20,350	53,098	-32,749
Maria Richie Leonard	1	4,013	50,542	-46,529
Kristina Sosa	2	23,272	73,191	-49,918
Denis Byron Espinoza	1	6,475	57,467	-50,992
Jerold McConnell	2	12,552	69,848	-57,296

If this were your team, cutting the bottom five originators would add $250,000 to the bottom line by avoiding their losses. That's the value of focus on contribution margin. The loan officer or AE with the highest contribution margin for a period of time wins first place. Note that loan volume is not considered. Why? Volume matters to loan officers and AEs because that's usually how they are paid. What matters to lenders?

I use contribution margin as the most direct measurement of profit at the loan officer, branch and TPO level. It measures the revenue produced by the loan officer, branch and TPO using the pricing provided to the originator. It subtracts all of the costs of obtaining the particular loan, including commission, salary, incentives, cures and concessions. I exclude allocations of any kind, because the originator can't control allocations. They can only control their loan quality, units produced at required margin and the compensation paid to them. This is similar to measuring the 'on base percentage' of a baseball player. How often do they get on base, and at what cost?

In the movie, Billy Beane asks, "How do we score runs?" The answer was always, "Get on base." How does a lender make money? Close loans with a high contribution margin. How does a lender make superior profitability? Close loans with a high contribution margin, with no defects, *and* with outstanding customer service.

Executives and Managers in mortgage lending are not very good at terminating poor performers. Just like Beane, we would be asking executives to work against instinct. "He or she will turn it around," you hear all the time. "It's a tough market." "His or her volume may be low, but it helps cover overhead." "He or she has had a tough time learning our system."

There's a scene in "Moneyball" where Beane orders his second in command Peter Brand to cut an underperforming player. Brand agonizes over the cut. Finally, he walks in and uses the script that Beane suggested. Two sentences, similar to "This isn't working out. Joe (personnel manager) will go over the paperwork." The meeting ends, and the player being cut simply says "OK," and empties his locker. It was just a business decision.

I've agonized over terminating poor performers, finding excuses to delay what I knew needed to be done. A great mentor, George

Brubaker, took me aside one day and said, "Jim, did you ever fire anyone and a week or so later think, "Wow, I shouldn't have fired him or her?" I said, "No." He then asked, "Jim, did you ever fire someone and think, "Wow, I should've done that a long time ago?" I said, "All the time." He then gave me George's rule: "The first time you ever think of firing someone, just do it." It's hard to do, but it's one of the best coaching elements I've ever been given.

And don't stop at production personnel from a data-driven perspective. One could do the same for processors, underwriters, closers, and other employees. One could track their hits, defect-free loan, with the lowest cost, with outstanding customer service. We could track their errors; cure costs, unhappy customers, concessions, unsalable loans, etc.

One could do the same for branches. (We'll cover all of these roles a little later in the book.)

DATA AND THE LENDER

Let's think more broadly about data. What data is in your possession that could be worth millions of contribution profit margin if properly deployed? Ms. Casanueva expanded her discussion on data:

> "The data-driven lender of the future will harness more and more data that is at their fingertips: The average loan origination system contains over 10,000 data fields. Servicing systems have payment histories, default, and foreclosure. Credit repositories have details of payment history. Appraisal management firms have appraisal data and transaction history on homes sold. The Realtor Multiple Listing Service has listing and sale information. Title insurers have the details of the title chain of properties. Verification services (like

the Work Number) have employment histories of borrowers. Fannie and Freddie have the whole ecosphere of data – borrower data, AUS findings, appraisal data sets, collateral histories. And there's more data in places one might not even think about. Banking demands deposit accounts – liquidity and deposit history for loans based upon bank statements. Social media contains self-contributed data about where one lives, family, significant events such as marriages, births, new employment, travel."

You get the idea. So, a little later, we will meld Data-Driven Lending with the Six Levers to suggest a path to *superior profitability, outstanding customer satisfaction, and defect-free loans.*

Let's dive further into Data-Driven Lending. Data-Driven Lending has to begin with a discussion on data integrity. "Dirty data" or missing data is responsible for much of the rework and underlying defects in mortgage banking. Ms. Casanueva observed:

"Data integrity in mortgage banking is a far cry from what it should be. The amount of missing or erroneous data throughout the process can cause major reductions in profitability. As we review data in lender systems, the basics seem to be there, but a close review still reveals data integrity issues in computation of income, in computation of liquid reserves, and missing ancillary data.

I'm surprised how dirty data can be. The root cause of much missing and 'dirty' data is the manual efforts in mortgage banking. These manual efforts need to be replaced with a data-driven approach to quality. Second to data integrity is the poor quality of operational and financial performance data. Many lenders don't key in on the key drivers of profitability and attainment of service levels."

APPLYING A DATA-DRIVEN STRATEGY TO THE SIX LEVERS

A Data-Driven Lender knows their own data and that of their peers. Peer data provides a way to judge "how well are we doing" in a factual and confidential manner. The Mortgage Bankers Association publishes a quarterly Mortgage Banking Profitability Report. The Report contains aggregated data for several hundred lenders. This data is very powerful for benchmarking and for understanding the intersection between the six levers of strategy and profit.

Readers may own or work for independent mortgage bankers of various sizes, or for depository lenders. There are distinct characteristics of each type of lender that affect both strategy and profit potential. We'll examine a variety of summary mortgage banking metrics in the following pages.

The metrics are broken into the type of lender. "Banks" include commercial banks and thrifts engaged in mortgage banking directly or through a subsidiary. "Independent Mortgage Bankers" are non-depository lenders engaged primarily in mortgage banking activities and are owned either publicly or by private shareholders. "Other" includes subsidiaries of non-depository institutions; hedge funds or hedge fund subsidiaries and REITs.

We examined product profitability above, and there are certainly excellent peer statistics published by MBA. When using the Six Levers method, choose the statistics that are relevant to the strategy.

To do this, consider using some of the following suggestions to start:

Economies of Scale

While size doesn't matter per se (see above), what does matter is how well a lender reaches economies of scale given their strategic choice of an appropriate scale. For example, if a lender could focus on FHA lending, develop the expertise to master FHA, become outstanding at understanding the credit characteristics and loan performance, one will have a thriving and profitable business built on scale in FHA lending.

A lender I worked with focused on FHA. The lender understood the demographics of their customers, their cultural habits, and understood the value of a home to their particular demographic. This lender was a GNMA issuer, so the lender could tailor their credit offerings without corresponding overlays. The result was a business line that had economies of scale, ranging from well-trained loan officers, well-trained DE underwriters, a credit risk function that reviewed credit trends, and a following of realtors who knew the lender could deliver. Size-wise, the lender closed about 3,000 loans per year. Profitability-wise, it was 100+ basis points every quarter.

The statistics that mattered to this lender were contribution margin per loan, processing cost per closed loan, underwriting cost per closed loan, pull through percentage with and without concessions, pre-closing finding per loan, credit performance of all loans, comparison statistics from FHA, market share of FHA loans in served markets, available via HMDA data, contribution margin of other types of loans, realtor referral statistics, time to commitment, and time to close. Economies of scale are not loan volume related per se, as described above.

Channels of Distribution

Lenders have to consider the profitability of channels of production. The TPO channel generally shifts the cost risk of production to TPO originators from lenders. One can examine the profitability of each channel over time and also the impact of product mix on the channel.

One peer measurement that is more difficult to find is direct-to-consumer profitability. Quicken's Rocket Mortgage legitimized direct-to-consumer as a viable channel. Previously, direct to consumer had a heavy refinance element to it. Loan officer commissions were lower, lead conversion was a key skill. Rocket Mortgage claims 'push button – get mortgage.' What Rocket really accomplishes is getting an opportunity to compete for purchase business, while putting tremendous pressure on retail originators and brokers.

A cynic told me Rocket should say 'push button – crush margins' because consumers can now get a legitimate rate quote from a reputable lender that has demonstrably outstanding customer service.

Realtors and retail loan officers may dismiss 'direct to consumer' for purchase lending because of the perceived control of borrowers in face-to-face situations. Realtors and retail loan officers will find the quote from Princess Leia to Darth Vader in "Star Wars," paraphrased: "The tighter your grip, the looser your grasp". As much as Realtors and Retail Loan Officers try to control customer decision making, the more Rocket and similar direct-to-consumer lenders loosen the face to face grasp. Watch cost to originate, sales commissions, and contribution margins in retail. Direct-to-consumer is a clear and present danger to the retail channel. The only apparent long run strategy for face to face originations is to develop a compelling relationship model that transcends a single transaction with a customer. For example, larger banks are using very competitive jumbo loans to attract customers into a long-term wealth management relationship with the bank. The jumbo is a marketing tool, sometimes priced with little or no transaction margin. If you are a transactional based lender, you lose this jumbo segment.

Another channel not considered as a direct to consumer channel is servicing recapture. Servicers that monetize the equity in their borrowers' home have a very good opportunity to provide rehab, remodeling, college funds, and other legitimate uses of equity from a very advantaged seat.

Technological and Process Transformation

I won't spend much time here, as my prior book covers this topic in detail. You can delve into these ideas at length by exploring 'Digital Transformation.'

Product Niche or Niches

Niches have always been great profit opportunities. Rehab, Construction to Perm, Fix/Flip, and Investor are excellent opportunities. Second lien and HELOC, bridge, and swing loans are also great opportunities. Depositories have a leg up on IMBs here due to portfolio capability. Banks should seriously look at the margins in these products, as direct to consumer opportunities as well as partnering with aggressive and competent IMBs.

Diversification

One can diversify via channels or product niches as described above or by looking at parallel markets. Homeowners' insurance, especially for servicers or large bank portfolios, second lien, small commercial, acquisition, construction and development financing, and partnering with builders and/or realtors on guaranteed sales programs all hold promise. A specific example is CMG Financial's "All in One" loan is a demand deposit account coupled to a line of credit aimed at helping a customer manage their cash flow and interest costs in a dynamic manner.

Relationship and Empathy Emphasis

Hard to do, but very rewarding for all parties if done well. Human relationships and Empathy are very difficult to incorporate into pure technology. Leveraging technology to provide the emotional connection of "you know me, care about me, and listen to me" is hard. One can do it by shifting the focus of employees from performing routine work to focusing on relationship building, and/or by using technology to augment the customer feelings, of "Hey, you know about me and are listening to my needs."

INDUSTRY PERFORMANCE METRICS

Let's analyze recent industry data and discuss which of the six levers might be a control for each metric of lender performance. The most important metric is profitability, so let's start there.

Product Profitability touches the levers of channels of distribution, technology and process transformation, product niches, and relationship and empathy.

As I spoke with readers of "Digitally Transforming the Mortgage Banking Industry," there was one chart and related discussion that received more comments than any other element of that book. I'm repeating that section here because it ties in so well to the issue of Strategy:

Let's first consider $1 billion in production for a moment. This is a hypothetical chart of four product types, each with $1 billion of production. Each amount is directionally accurate, but not intended to be precise. This chart is a summary snapshot of the financial elements of the value chain. Originator compensation and operational labor are held at a constant unit rate for simplicity. Jim MacLeod noted that "lenders need to focus on segments, not the market as a whole. Focus on profit, not volume." The takeaway is that different products have meaningfully different gross margins, with gross margin defined as revenue less direct costs of origination and operations but excluding overhead. For illustrative purposes, the chart below shows the extreme—what gross margin would be if one originated just a single product set. The following page shows an example of how a lender might target a specific gross margin strategy.

Loan Mix Analysis

	JUMBO	HIGH BALANCE	CONVENTIONAL	GOVIE
ANNUAL PRODUCTION	$1,000,000,000	$1,000,000,000	$1,000,000,000	$1,000,000,000
AVERAGE LOAN BALANCE	$750,000	$550,000	$250,000	$175,000
UNITS	1,333	1,818	4,000	5,714
NET MARGIN	2.5%	2.25%	3.4%	4.5%
GAIN ON SALE	25,000,000	22,500,000	34,500,000	45,000,000
ORIGINATOR COMP AND BENEFITS	$11,000,000	$11,000,000	$11,000,000	$11,000,000
PRICING CONCESSIONS	1,000,000	1,250,000	750,000	200,000
DIRECT LABOR OPERATIONAL COST	3,466,667	4,727,273	10,400,000	14,857,143
GROSS MARGIN	$9,533,333	$5,522,727	$12,350,000	$18,942,856

For instance, if a lender wanted a high degree of FHA and VA loans, the lender may focus on geographies that have a high concentration of FHA and VA business opportunities. Working on the operational cost side, underwriters are costlier in major coastal metro areas, versus other smaller cities. I've had numerous discussions on locating operations centers in lower cost geographies, and the numbers speak for themselves. One California based lender was amazed by the cost impact of expanding its operational functions into a mid-west city. "Skilled operational labor is 30-45% less costly, and I don't have to worry about underwriters and other skilled operational people moving around every six months looking for more money as they do in California." These financial decisions regarding base level costs matter, as do operational efficiency and product mix.

I'm not aware of any mortgage banker that failed because of lack of volume. Failure of independent mortgage bankers is often a function of lack of profit and liquidity, not volume. Depository lenders seem to get in trouble from too much volume that doesn't translate into profitable operations.

PULL-THROUGH

The ratio of applications taken to closed loans is known as pull-through. This is a Process Transformation Lever. Why? We measure pull-through in general, and it appears that it hasn't changed much over the years. The ratio of loans completed versus loans started, or pull-through, is one of them. The following chart shows pull-through by year, by type of lender. Thus, the costs incurred in originating loans hasn't been affected by increases in fallout[51], meaning working on loans that never close. Higher fallout adversely affects productivity. The key metric missing in the statistics below is "pull-through with price/fee concessions" and "pull-through without price/fee concessions." That data isn't available from MBA statistics, but it's very important as concessions represent reduced profitability on a loan. If you are not tracking pull-through with and without price and fee concessions, you may be missing extremely powerful data.

Some observers attribute higher recent pull-through in banks due to the availability of portfolio loan products, especially jumbos as well as the propensity for depository lenders to express a wider credit box for Community Reinvestment Act eligible loans. In any event, loans that don't close are a very real cost that needs to be managed. These pull-through statistics are from Application to Closing. The statistics do not consider personnel and other costs spent on leads that never make an application.

Pull-Through % versus Fall-Out Rate (by Lender Type)

Source: MBA Mortgage Bankers
Performance Report

PULL THROUGH ●—●
FALL OUT ●┄●

BANK

73.7	73.4	74.9	77	76.5	74.7

26.3	26.6	25.1	23	23.5	25.3

2012	2013	2014	2015	2016	2017

IMB

72.9	73.8	74.5	73.2	72.6	74.1

27.1	26.2	25.5	26.8	27.4	25.9

2012	2013	2014	2015	2016	2017

OTHER

71.2	71.8	71.8	74.1	71	72.6

28.8	28.2	28.2	25.9	29	27.4

2012	2013	2014	2015	2016	2017

This is a Process Transformation Lever because of what traditional pull-through doesn't measure. It doesn't measure pull-through with and without price concessions. Remember the earlier discussion on product and process profitability. Just like Billy Beane coaching batters, concessions to keep a loan is like giving up an out. You do the loan, but don't make the expected profit contribution margin. Pull-through measurement without managing concessions is a correctable source of profit leakage.

Staffing and Unit Volume

Source: MBA Mortgage Bankers Performance Report

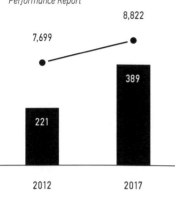

AVERAGE TOTAL LOAN UNITS	●━●
TOTAL EMPLOYEES	■■■

Employee Productivity: this is an Economies of Scale and a Technology and Process Transformation Lever's look at employee productivity, since we know pull-through has remained relatively constant. The average lender has increased employment by 76% from 2012 to 2017, but lender loan volume by units has grown by 15%. Thus, there appears to be a productivity gap that is pushing cost to produce upward. As many CEOs interviewed have noted, there are a lot more "checkers checking the checkers;" thus, a large productivity gap over the last five years.

As questioned earlier, does loan volume lead to profitability? A certain level of volume is, of course, necessary to achieve sufficient economies of scale and offset some of the reduced productivity caused by substantially increased regulatory costs noted above. Some may believe that annual production in the range of $500 million appears to be the level necessary to support sufficient economies of scale. In fact, as set out in the accompanying chart that follows, lenders with less than $200 million of originations have been consistently profitable. Volume does not equate to profit. A given lender's $1 billion in originations may or may not be profitable. In fact, in any given quarter over the past five years, 10-20% of the reporting lenders were not profitable. Rather than pursuing this steadfast dedication to volume, lenders should instead focus on maximizing profit.

Are there efficiencies with larger lenders, looking at average closing per production and fulfillment employees? The answer is a qualified yes, though the results may include the impact of more efficient consumer direct channels in the larger lenders that are combined with traditional retail. The distribution of monthly closing by sales employee in recent years is not significantly different by lender. Recall that 2012 experienced significant refinance volume; the higher productivity of sales employees in 2012 and 2013 may have been related to servicing recapture activities of larger lenders, as well as direct to consumer refinance activities skewing results in 2012 and 2013. As volume is more purchase-oriented, the productivity differences do not appear as material. Nonetheless, it is clear that productivity has declined substantially since 2012, and the borrower is bearing these costs.

Monthly Closings per Sales Employee

Source: MBA Mortgage Bankers Performance Report

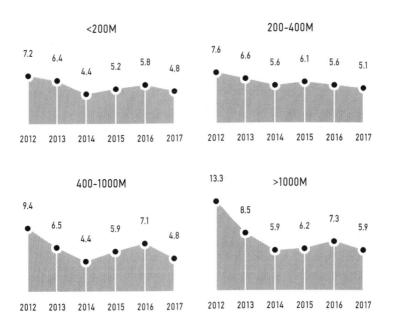

JAMES M. DEITCH CPA, CMB

ORIGINATION CHANNEL PROFITABILITY

The next area to consider is channel of origination, a strategic lever in and of itself. The chart below compares profitability for each channel: predominantly retail, a mix of retail and wholesale, and predominantly wholesale.

Interestingly, the channel mix for all periods was profitable. The retail channel is generally the most profitable and includes consumer direct. Consumer direct is not separated from traditional retail, so it is not clear whether the retail is lifted by the generally much higher profitability of consumer direct business. What is also clear is that the increasing costs of origination noted above are being passed onto the consumer. Over the course of the past six years, loan origination activity had produced about 50 basis points of pretax profit, despite the reduction in productivity noted above.

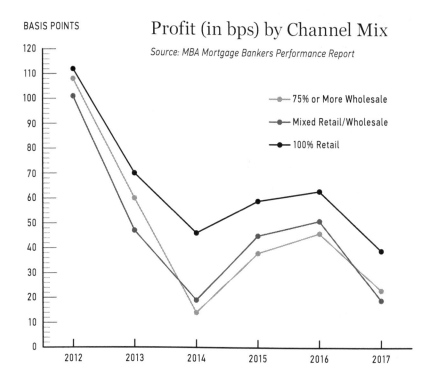

Profit (in bps) by Channel Mix

Source: MBA Mortgage Bankers Performance Report

BASIS POINTS

75% or More Wholesale
Mixed Retail/Wholesale
100% Retail

This leads to several conclusions. First, the cost of regulation is very real, and contrary to the public comments by high profile regulators, the consumer is paying a lot of money for the so-called consumer protections promulgated by a variety of federal and state regulators. All lenders are subject to the increased regulatory cost load, and it is simply passed on. Second, the reduced productivity *coupled with* relatively low technology spend suggests that substantial productivity increases are possible. Third, the lenders that quickly achieve substantial productivity increases will see that *most of that productivity falling right to the bottom line.* If a lender becomes much more efficient than most competitors, the reduced costs drop right to the bottom line.

This is evident for a variety of reasons mentioned above, as well as because the GSEs have not differentiated guarantee fees based on volume as they had pre-crisis. The playing field is level right now regarding GSEs. Dave Stevens cites increased competition and level playing field access to GSEs as key elements of GSE reform.

PRODUCT MIX AND PROFITABILITY

Mix is a product niche lever. Does product mix affect profitability? The chart below sets out profitability by Government Loans and Conventional Loans. These two loan types account for 95% of the volume of originations in the relevant years.[52] The gross revenue by loan type varies, but clearly, lenders that

Profit (in bps) by Loan Type Mix

Source: MBA Mortgage Bankers Performance Report

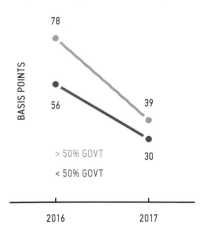

concentrate on GSE conventional lending have lower revenues and significantly lower profitability. That effect is particularly evident in the several quarters as set out below. This is a real-world illustration of the first chart that illustrated relative profitability by loan mix.

So, in summary, a few take-aways:

- Size of the lender does not matter as much as other factors, such as efficiency, product mix, and channel.

- All the information cited above are averages among hundreds of lenders. Actual lender data varies considerably. For instance, in any given period, 10-20 percent of lenders report that they were unprofitable for a given quarter.

- Productivity increases appear to offer lenders the opportunity to achieve substantial increases in profitability. Productivity increases include both the sales and fulfillment areas.

- More significantly, though, is the simple fact that volume does not equate to profit. Any given $1 billion in originations may or may not be profitable. Rather than pursuing this steadfast dedication to volume, lenders should, instead, focus on profit per loan.

- Laser focus on the value chain can drive origination pre-tax profits to 100+ basis points.

REVENUE AND COST BY ACTIVITY

Revenue and Cost by Activity is a Technology and Process Transformation Lever. Below is a conceptual model[42] for managing the value chain, with its revenue and expense components interposed within the culture and experience dimensions of the value chain. The revenue and cost associated with each activity is set out below.

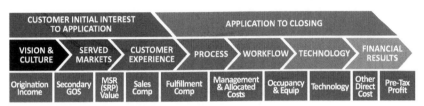

Here is the cost stack for this model with data over the years:

LOAN PRODUCTION EXPENSES	2015		2016		2017	
Sales Personnel	$2,690	38.2%	$2,711	37.6%	$2,971	36.8%
Fulfillment Personnel	2,009	28.5%	2,091	29.0%	2,376	29.4%
Occupancy and Equipment	380	5.4%	358	5.0%	435	5.4%
Technology-Related Expenses	131	1.9%	141	2.0%	172	2.1%
Outsourcing and Professional Fees	286	4.1%	260	3.6%	264	3.3%
Other Operating Expenses	1,156	16.4%	1,252	17.4%	1,303	16.1%
Direct Loan Production Expenses	$6,652	94.4%	$6,812	94.5%	$7,521	93.0%
Corporate Allocation	394	5.6%	396	5.5%	562	7.0%
Total Cost to Produce	$7,046	100.0%	$7,208	100.0%	$8,083	100.0%

Source: MBA Mortgage Bankers Performance Report

The Customer Initial Interest to Application phase is largely driven by Vision, Culture, Served Market Selection, and the desired Customer Experience. This is market positioning – it's the look and feel of a lender.

---

[42] This model was introduced in "Digitally Transforming the Mortgage Banking Industry" as is repeated here as many executives commented favorably on this mental model for clarifying their thinking.

JAMES M. DEITCH CPA, CMB

If the lender's positioning and value proposition are attractive to a prospective customer, the customer makes an application, completing the revenue portion of the sale. At this point, the loan application is priced, fees are set, and servicing value and gain on sale are fixed. It's very likely that this is the best that the revenue stream is going to get with this customer, due to a variety of consumer protection laws and regulations.

Said another way, if everything is well-managed and occurs according to plan, the revenue side of the loan will be realized. Hedging may augment the economic value of the loan, but these activities are purely financial gains unrelated to customer service.

The Application to Closing path is where the Customer Experience is confirmed or altered. It's also where the anticipated profit is ultimately earned or leaked away. Process, Workflow, and Technology shepherd the loan from Application through Closing. The experience continues through loan boarding and servicing over time, but we'll stop at closing for the loan origination value chain analysis for now. The Application to Closing is also where much profit is lost.

What I have seen in many lenders is that an analysis of expected profitability along the value chain at consumer lock, compared to realized profitability at investor funding, has many revenue and profit leakage points[53]. A loan-level examination of profit from consumer lock to funding is a very effective data discovery project. One can see 10, 20, 30, 50 basis points of profit lost along the way. If you haven't reconciled expected profitability at the loan level to actual loan funding by an investor, you are likely missing a rich source for finding and plugging these leaks. Lenders that make 100+ basis points have a materially lower level of leaks compared to less profitable peers.

Let's examine the value chain more closely using 2017 peer data for a generic IMB peer. The peer data is horizontal, in the same direction of the value chain for comparison purposes.

Origination Income	Secondary GOS	MSR (SRP) Value	Sales Comp	Fulfillment Comp	Management & Allocated Costs	Occupancy & Equip	Technology	Other Direct Cost	Pre-Tax Profit
77	218	100	154	65	45	20	8	72	30
395 BASIS POINTS			365 BASIS POINTS						

Source: MBA Mortgage Bankers Performance Report

Origination Income includes fees retained by the lender and not passed on to third parties; Gain on Sale is net of hedge costs and gains; MSR value is the value of Mortgage Servicing Rights if retained or the Servicing Release Premium ("SRP") if sold; Sales compensation includes commissions, benefits, salaries, overrides and bonuses for originators, sales assistants, and origination management; Fulfillment compensation includes operational costs of closing a loan including compensation, benefits, and bonuses for operational and operations management; Management includes senior management and allocated costs such as corporate overhead; Technology includes LOS and other technology costs excluding compensation; Other Direct Costs includes secondary, post-closing, quality control ("QC"), and non-recovered third-party costs.

PROFITABILITY BY ENTITY AND CHANNEL

Consider benchmarking your own results against these 2017 statistics for additional insights into your lending results. Channel and Entity Profitability affects the Channel and Diversification levers.

Using this model, we can then analyze the revenue and expense stack of a variety of operating options. For example, we can look at Bank, IMB, and Other lender groups by component of revenue or cost. The relative cost of sales compensation can be seen as the major driver of cost base by lender type.

Revenue/Expense (in bps) by Lender Type

Source: MBA Mortgage Bankers Performance Report

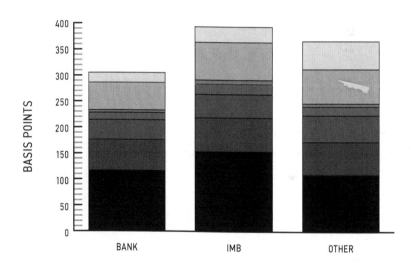

Loan size also drives performance. Consider that loan size is both geographically driven as well as driven by loan type. FHA loans are generally smaller than conventional ones and carry higher margins.

The impact of loan type and geography appear interrelated on the loan size graph below. Compensation for operational elements declines by loan size as expected. Larger loans do not experience a commensurate increase in effort from operational employees. In some cases, it might be argued larger conventional loans require less effort, as the credit box of GSE loan vintages in recent years are very tight, so the expected operational effort would be lower.

Revenue/Expense (in bps) by Loan Size

Source: MBA Mortgage Bankers Performance Report

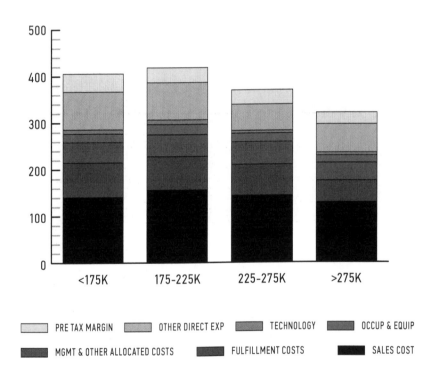

The results by lender size suggest that each lender group has a revenue and cost structure that supports the model. Notable among smaller lenders is sales compensation. This factor may be due to self-production of loans by ownership, with compensation being realized as profitability as opposed to sales commission. Fulfillment costs, Management costs, and Other Direct costs for larger lenders appear smaller per loan, likely the result of some economies of scale.

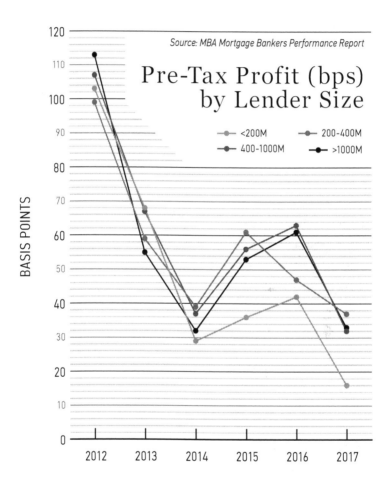

The Revenue Stack for lender size is different, likely reflecting a pure best effort strategy for smaller lenders, with a more sophisticated hedging strategy leading to increased revenue for larger lenders.

The largest lenders likely have third-party channels included, which reduce both revenue and cost. All in all, it is remarkable that a small lender and a large lender are both profitable, with an 21-basis point spread in profit suggesting scale is not a driving factor in origination profit at this point in time.

Said another way, culture, strategy, and customer experience seem to be the driving force for profitability, not loan volume. Larger lenders have larger absolute profitability, but it is important that a smaller lender can earn an acceptable profit in the current market.

The impact of channel selection is much more apparent in the graph below. The channel breakout for consumer direct versus retail represents a small sample, so the extension of these results should be cautioned. Consumer direct channels that I have observed tend to have a much higher profitability than the amounts listed below. The third-party origination ("TPO") wholesale channel appears representative, with lower revenue, due to broker compensation, and costs, paid by the broker, shifting the overall revenue and cost structure, but still resulting in profitable operations. In some respects, the TPO shifting of the cost structure onto brokers could represent a more easily scalable and de-scalable business model as demand fluctuates.

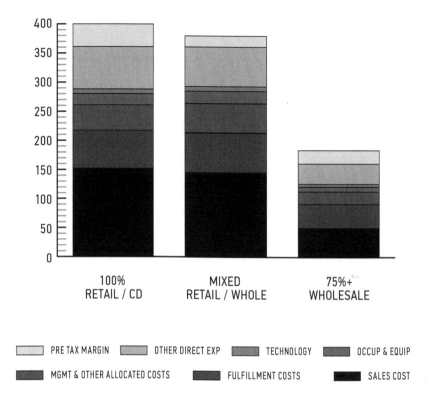

PRE TAX MARGIN	OTHER DIRECT EXP
TECHNOLOGY	OCCUP & EQUIP
MGMT & OTHER ALLOCATED COSTS	FULFILLMENT COSTS
SALES COST	

Finally, product mix profitability is apparent by FHA/VA mix. Higher profitability is apparent in the higher FHA/VA mix. Some of the most profitable origination models are structured towards FHA/VA lending in secondary and tertiary geographies, or in consumer direct models focusing on FHA/VA product, though these operations have a higher refinance component, and it is not clear whether these models can translate into a primarily purchase driven model. The following chart shows FHA/VA percentage mix:

Revenue/ Expenses (in BPS) by Product Mix

Source: MBA Mortgage Bankers Performance Report

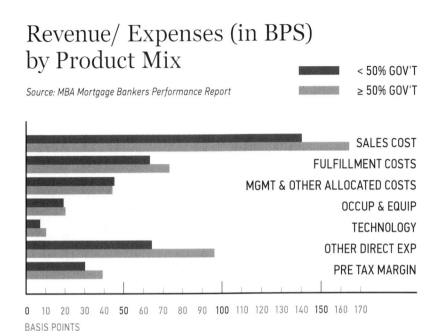

Legend:
- < 50% GOV'T
- ≥ 50% GOV'T

Categories:
SALES COST
FULFILLMENT COSTS
MGMT & OTHER ALLOCATED COSTS
OCCUP & EQUIP
TECHNOLOGY
OTHER DIRECT EXP
PRE TAX MARGIN

0 10 20 30 40 50 60 70 80 90 100 110 120 130 140 150 160 170
BASIS POINTS

Lastly, from an industry perspective, it is hard to justify the labor cost in mortgage banking, both in sales and in fulfillment employees. Productivity hasn't increased over the past six years. In fact, it's gotten worse because employee compensation costs have risen but throughput hasn't. Said another way, each fulfillment employee labor effort closes six loans per month.

That's about three and a half days of fulfillment labor to close one mortgage loan. By contrast, General Motors builds a Buick SUV with about two-thirds the amount of union labor. Imagine that GM can manufacture a car with less labor than it takes a lender to manufacture a stack of paper for a loan. This model doesn't appear to be sustainable.

Monthly Closings
per Fulfillment Employee

Source: MBA Mortgage Bankers Performance Report

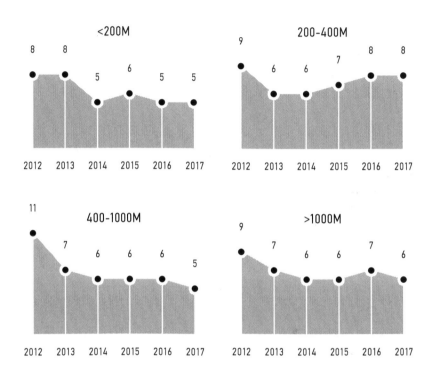

CHAPTER 6

THE MAVERICKS' HANDS ON APPROACH TO STRATEGIC TRANSFORMATION

Progress on a data-driven Strategic Transformation often runs into a buzz saw of organizational roadblocks. From legacy systems to the personality quirks of senior management, you've probably encountered numerous challenges. The following are some thoughts on how to plow through such roadblocks and make steady progress towards your Strategic Transformation with a Maverick's approach.

AIM HIGH

While parsing all of this, I think it's important to keep some words of wisdom in mind, once again from Billy Beane. When implementing your hands-on approach to Strategic Transformation, lead from the top. As Billy put it:

> *"We apply data driven decision making with discipline and consistency. Discipline starts at the leadership level. The*

discipline needs to be adopted throughout the organization.
Discipline and consistency are required at all levels of an
organization, from the CEO to front line."

Debbie Dunn of SWBC spoke of the biggest challenge in success
with technology. "Loan officer and employee adoption of new
technology can be a struggle. The natural tendency is to continue
to do things the 'old way'. That creates inefficiencies. Adoption has
to be a requirement, not an option."

Why does our industry find 20 basis points of pretax profit on
origination as acceptable? It's a result of accepting such results as
inevitable in a seasonal, cyclical commodity business like mortgage
banking. But one doesn't have to accept the 'commodity' part of
the description. Yes, mortgage banking is seasonal and cyclical, but
it's a business choice to treat it as a commodity.

Several CEOs I spoke with expressed their profit goals as a threshold
for adequate return. "You've got to aim high," one CEO told me.
"It's harder to attain a mediocre goal than assemble a team committed to making a very tough goal."

Further illustrating this, yet another CEO of a high performing
mortgage banker said in conversation, "100 basis points + of pretax
return is the target for my origination business. That's my hurdle
rate for making business decisions." Interestingly, that CEO has
achieved that target four years running.

That laser focus on 100+ basis points of profit transcended volume,
but it did not transcend customer experience.

"We focus on our desired customer segments and deliver on our
promised customer experience. My entire team is aligned with

the desired experience and our focus on our desired customer segments. Our model works. Sometimes volume is higher, sometimes lower, but we manage for 100 basis points plus every year."

This CEO is intently dialed into the power of aiming high.

Rose Marie David of HomeStreet related to aiming high when performing Strategic Transformation:

> *"We've been working on strategic transformation for the past 18 months. We had to rationalize branches with high jumbo concentration markets where you're competing with the national money centers banks. We have to focus on core markets where we offer a strong product mix.*
>
> *We've made tough decisions on loan officers and fulfillment personnel that did not quite meet our performance and service level standards. We've honed our processes and increased our loan quality. All of this is painful and takes time to do well. The reward is we're so much further along on strategic transformation.*
>
> *We set high standards, and we expect team members to meet them."*

The benefits of aiming high result in a culture of high expectations, which sustains the transformation achieved.

JUST SAY 'NO' TO DOCTOR NO

A CEO committed to Strategic Transformation related a particular frustration with his Chief Information Officer. "I talk with my CIO on the data and system requirements for strategic transformation, and I run into a brick wall. My CIO has a nickname: 'Dr. No.' Whatever the ask, the answer is 'no'. I'd fire him, but I don't have a better candidate at this moment. Meanwhile, little progress."

This love/hate relationship with a CIO, and other Senior Managers, is a very common feeling with C-level executives. One of the root causes of 'Dr. No' syndrome is that lenders must deal with legacy systems. Most servicing systems trace their roots back to the computer mainframe days of the 1990s. Core banking systems have similar parentage. Most loan origination systems have newer architecture, but their functional DNA dates back to the 1930s and the establishment of FHA and Fannie Mae. Customer front-ends such as Blend, Roostify, and BeSmartee make the customer experience at the heart of the industry easier, but these systems are also limited in their data reach into other systems.

Many senior managers also subscribe to what I call the "Big Bang" theory of technology. The "Big Bang" is that we can't do anything until we can do everything. Legacy system dependencies thoroughly complicate forward progress on anything, leading inevitably to 'Dr. No' syndrome.

Dr. No's come in all sizes and shapes, but there are ways of handling them. One CEO handles 'Dr. No's with a question, "Under what circumstances could we accomplish my request, what would it cost, and how long would it take?" This question usually produces a more reflective answer and some forward momentum.

Some 'Dr. No' employees are simply hardwired to be very conservative in their approach, however. These are great employees in Internal Audit and other control positions. But 'Dr. No' has no place in a key line management position. Don't let a Dr. No serve as a roadblock to your Strategic Transformation. As my friend George Brubaker said, "Fire the employee the first time you think of it."

JAMES M. DEITCH CPA, CMB

BABY STEPS TO BIG DATA

On a shorter term basis, a CEO can take a Strategic Transformation approach to their business by liberating their data from legacy systems and having a roadmap in place to achieve their Strategic Transformation. This, by definition, involves small, cautious moves forward— so-called 'baby steps.' The value of leveraging data-driven analysis in tandem with baby steps is critical for true Strategic success.

Jonathan Corr of Ellie Mae Inc. describes his strategic roadmap for data liberation via the Encompass LOS:

> *"We want to make all of the data within Encompass available to a lender. Standard fields, custom fields, virtual fields. Everything. We will provide such data access with DataConnect. This provides a lender with direct access to their data to use within an Enterprise Data Lake. The lender can use it in conjunction with a data science workbench. The data can be combined with servicing data, loan performance data. The Encompass platform is the backbone for a lender's data."*

Maylin Casanueva of Teraverde described her thinking on getting at lender data creatively and quickly through baby steps:

> *"LOS data, servicing data, due diligence data, quality assurance data, loan officer compensation data, company service level data, legacy documents from origination through servicing can all be accessed today. It's not easy, but APIs and other technology let us take baby steps to get this data into actionable data-driven intelligence.*

This data is the key to data-driven strategic transformation. For example, we've helped a lender match the loan level credit box at origination, quality assurance findings to loan performance through servicing, loss mitigation, and risk management activities. And we are matching every employee or TPO that touched each loan, their service levels, and the ultimate performance of each loan by employee. We can see the variation of performance of each employee compared to the service level attainment and loan performance outcome.

These baby steps lead to better credit decisions and loan performance. More importantly, the lender can see the impact that individual employees have on loan performance, loan defects, customer satisfaction, and loan level profitability. Joining a variety of structured and unstructured data provides data-driven actionable intelligence."

Mary Aston, an executive with Angel Oak spoke of her success in using 'baby steps':

"Data driven decision-making is an important element of our business. The most important first step is to make sure the data is accurate and complete. Data Integrity is the biggest issue in the industry, and it takes a lot of careful planning to get the data right.

The industry spends so much effort cleaning up data after the fact. Checkers checking checkers as opposed to generating trusted data at every step of the lending process. We are investing in strategic transformation of the end-to-end lending process, from origination to securitization. We already see the lift in data quality, and the return on investment on data integrity is very high."

Nima Ghamsari, CEO of Blend, has similar views on the small steps that can yield big results:

> *"I think the biggest, the hardest part.... there's always this Nirvana view of the future, of 'here's how good this could be if we solved all these problems at once.' That has two sorts of pitfalls to it that I think are worth thinking about for companies that are undergoing this journey. The first is not every problem has been solved by companies that are out there. There's a long way to go. There's a lot more to solve. And the industry is enormous. There are so many participants. There are so many parts of the process."*

Meaning, that having a clear roadmap of the customer experience, process, and workflow lets one deploy solutions to the most pressing issues now and then undergo continuous improvement to reach the ultimate destination. So many projects fail by attempting to implement segments that are just too large.

> *"If we waited for everybody to solve all these things before we released our product, we'd be having this conversation in 2030. It would be a long time before we solved it. But also, what that means for the organization is that even within the organization they don't even need to use everything that we or others have to get started. So, by that I mean [some lenders] need everything integrated and everything perfect before I get started. But actually, the incremental value and the incremental benefit to your customers, if you're a financial institution, of getting something up and running that allows [customers] to get that simplicity and transparency is big enough on its own."*

"Constant improvement towards the right vision, towards that perfect Nirvana world that everyone wants… but don't wait for the Nirvana world before you make a move. It's critically important that the overall experience, process, and workflow be understood and documented so that the highest value technology components can be implemented first."

In other words, have a broad Strategic Transformation plan, but get the data at your fingertips right now.

BE RESULTS DRIVEN

Many of my peers note that many employees in the industry expect high compensation, especially commissioned salespeople, whether retail, wholesale or correspondent, and every issue or problem is the company's fault. One peer mentioned, "Loan officers want 40-50% of the gross revenue on a transaction, but don't have any responsibility for loan performance, compliance risk or errors that cost the company money." I asked how the lender measures loan officers. The answer: "By closed loan volume."

The company didn't have clear expectations on pull-through, concessions, cures, and turnaround time, nor on loan mix or loan officer service levels.

The CEO replied, "I can't measure all of that." Why not? "The LOS and other systems can't report it." My response to that? Set the expectations and find a way to measure performance. The conversation meandered to the key metric the CEO measured: loan volume.

My response: you are getting exactly what your expectation is; volume. You hired loan officers with only a volume mindset, and you continue to employ them without providing a clear expectation of all of the results expected of them.

The CEO was both pissed off and startled. "But I have to have them for volume."

That's a key mistake. The CEO's role is to create the conditions for success and create the clear and transparent goals of what is expected, and it's not just volume.

Creating an environment that is very transparent and oriented toward key performance metrics is central to this. Ultimately, when you put competitive people together in a transparent environment, it drives the entire organization to more profitable results.

Contrast these two direct-to-consumer operations. The first operation has large monitors in the sales area, showing each loan agent's unit and volume statistics, conversion ratio, and other metrics. Behind the scenes, the manager responsible for the operation focused on lead costs and how much profit was generated by each agent. Consider another direct-to-consumer operation. As I walked through the call center, the CEO mentioned to me that his "best" direct-to-consumer originator had over twice the volume of the nearest originator. The only metric displayed was agent volume and a 'gong' pull that signaled a lead conversion to a sale to all on the floor. A further review noted that his "best" agent's high level of sales resulted from a lead conversion ratio of one-third of the company average. The originator simply focused on the leads that he thought would be the easiest to fulfill, and he undermanaged the rest. End result: the "best" originator was actually one of the least profitable.

A corollary to transparency is to emphasize outcomes. A focus on outcomes helps employees differentiate activity from productivity. Being on the phone during a shift is activity. Activity may result in profitable operations. Productively converting leads to applications produces profit. Build a strategy focused on profit, not activity or volume.

Here's another example of activity versus productivity to consider. I once employed an assistant that had a way of complicating virtually everything. She would then complain that she always had to deal with problem people, problem vendors, etc. I asked her one morning, "What is your job?" She went on to list all the things she was working on. I looked her in the eye, and said, "No, your job is to make my life easier. You are not succeeding at that." She was surprised. "I don't need you to work here if you don't make my life easier." That simple conversation transformed her output. For several months, my conversation with her was, "What are you doing to make my life easier?" The happy results were productivity from goal alignment and simple focus, and she continued her employment.

TAKE PRUDENT RISKS

The brightening regulatory climate is encouraging some Mavericks to take prudent risks. Eddy Perez of Equity Prime took his cultural knowledge and developed a strategy to use Equity Prime's GNMA issuer capability to better serve borrowers:

> "When Equity Prime became a GNMA issuer, it's like we were promoted from the minor leagues to the majors. It gives you more ability to help borrowers. What's misunderstood about the Hispanic market is the commitment to maintain a home. I know it extremely well because I grew up 100 percent Cuban.

Lenders get caught up on ratios. Oftentimes, the calculation of DTI overstates the true family DTI. The Gig economy is real. Borrowers are making money doing extra jobs or they have family members who are contributing to the household and who are going to live there. So, you can look at a bank statement and determine if the cash flow is there to make the payment.

Why are these peoples' deposits so much higher than their reported income? You discover one or two family members that earn $3,000 a month. So, is the DTI really 52 or 38% with the extra liquid cash on bank statement deposits? When you're dealing with the aggregators they won't care if the people who have $100,000 in the bank get another $3,000 deposits because their 17-year-old kids are working. That's very common in the underserved market, especially in the Hispanic market. We can make those loans because we know they will perform. It's a prudent risk to take.

Matt Durkee of NBT stated that

"A bank can compute income for a portfolio loan to meet ATR standards and not get caught up in the 400 pages of GSE guidelines on computing income. The bank has the deposit history, and can use prudent, make-sense underwriting to help borrowers that don't fit neatly into the FannieMae documentation box."

Another prudent risk to take is expanding the voices that one engages with both in the company and within the industry. Marcia Davies of the MBA, who founded the mPower leadership group, explains further:

"The more diverse the group around the leadership table, the better the outcome. If you surround yourself with people who think like you and have the same background as you, you're probably going to come up with solutions that are in your comfort zone to tackle a problem or seize an opportunity. But if you look at it from different angles and consider different perspectives, the opportunity opens itself up for you to consider ways you otherwise wouldn't have had the insight and advantage to consider.

We formalized the mPower program to help expand opportunities for talented women. The growth has been so explosive. I'm hoping the network continues to expand. The number of women who tell me the benefits of the network has been overwhelming. Women are doing business and seeing business results by some of the connections that they have made in the network. They are able to mentor and coach others. The energy that comes out of events where women feel like they get some real time solutions to help them navigate in the workplace. So I would hope that our community would continue to grow and be strong and that we'll see more women rising in the ranks in this industry and more women represented on boards and more womens' voices around the table."

Eddy and Marcia have valuable perspectives that revolve around the power of relationship, empathy, and taking the risk to build relationships and show empathy broadly in the industry.

STOP REVENUE LEAKAGE

Revenue leakage touches almost all of the levers of strategy. Poor profitability has reached a crisis level. As we begin a comprehensive look at Data-Driven Profitability Management, we'll start with Revenue Leakage. I first wrote about Revenue Leakage in a March 2015 article of the same title in Mortgage Banking Magazine. The response from CEOs was strong. The response spawned much additional research and a series of approaches to get to the heart of revenue leakage. The sources of revenue leakage are varied and many.

Similar to the discussion above on being results driven, revenue leakage is a choice. A C-level executive needs to identify, measure, and assign revenue leakage to a specific individual that is responsible for each dollar of leakage. Once identified, each element of revenue leakage should be addressed by the responsible employee. Many employees express surprise at the dollar size and impact of revenue leakage items that they are responsible for.

Most employees desire to do a good job and perform well. Imagine the power of the organization to transform itself if each dollar of revenue leakage were identified and assigned to the employee responsible for the leakage. Not to assign blame; rather, to ask for suggestions on how to eliminate the leakage.

Some leakage arises from individual mistakes. These leakages are training related. Train the employee on the correct process and the leakage is reduced or eliminated. Some leakages arise from systemic issues. Systemic leakage, when corrected, has a powerful positive impact because the improvements are permanent.

An example: A long-term employee of a client walked into the CEO's office. The employee asks,

"Why can't our LOS auto-populate an underwriter's signature on certain FHA forms? I have to print the form, manually sign it, then scan it into the document folder. Our IT leader says it can't be done."

I thought, "Another Dr. No at a different company!" It turns out the signature could be automated, but the IT Director didn't know how to do it.

Once implemented by someone who did know how to do it, the employee walked back into the CEO's office. She gave the CEO a big hug. She said,

"That little bit of process automation saves about 15 minutes a file, by my calculations. That's about 700 hours per year in the department. And it removes a real dissatisfying process for our underwriting team. Thank you!"

Think of systemic leakages as 'designed-in profit reducers.' No leader would want to suggest that their processes have design flaws that shred profit dollars. But systemic flaws are exactly that: the process flaws shred dollars.

Why? Someone at some time designed the business process. The leakages are process design shortcomings. Why would someone design a process to have a manual step that requires an underwriter to print a document, sign it, and scan it back into the system? They wouldn't, meaning that most systemic process flaws are oversights or represent a lack of effort by process designers who have an imperfect understanding of mortgage banking.

Here is a partial list of revenue leakage items. Systemic, human error, or both?

- Uncollectable fees and repricings

- Cures for disclosure defects

- Price concessions on rate locks, float downs, and relocks

- Consumer concessions for goodwill

- Rework of loans due to workflow and business process defects

- Lock extensions required for investor funding stipulations not cured on a timely basis

- Unwillingness for an investor to fund a loan due to document defects, alleged underwriting, or compliance defects, etc.

- Guarantees and advances to loan officers and branches that fall short of projections

- Litigation and regulatory enforcement costs for process, disclosure, and other issues

The list could go on and on, really. What may help to illustrate how varied the complexities involved are is to walk through some real-life examples. In one scenario, a lender's pricing engine had errors in branch margin and loan level price adjusters. The result? Seven figures of revenue leakage.

LOAN SERVICING

My introduction to servicing was in 1989. Defaults were low. The servicer collected 25 basis points of the servicing fee, had the use of deposits when short-term rates were 7%, and the direct cost to service a loan was under $40 per loan. Life was straightforward, and servicing was a relatively simple asset.

Loan servicing used to be considered an effective offset to variations in production. When originations ebb, the servicing provides cash flow to offset the slower origination levels. When rates fall, refinance and recapture of servicing serve as the production hedge to offset servicing run-offs. The production hedge was an added bonus. At the time, one didn't capitalize self-generated servicing, and life truly was pretty straightforward.

The FASB unwittingly sowed the seeds for volatility in mortgage servicing rights assets, and more importantly, provided the fuel to generate the explosive growth of subprime mortgages. The ability to capitalize a future stream of income from subprime assets was a necessary ingredient for the growth of the segment. High relative interest rates and excess servicing fees could be capitalized to turn individual loans into valuable assets fetching pricing of 108, 109—the sky was the limit. Add aggressive estimates on loss ratios and prepayment penalties to prevent refinances, and a perfect storm was set in motion.

During the early 2000s, a few large correspondent lenders controlled a large segment of the servicing market. Then the crisis hit. Delinquencies increased. Strategic defaults hit the portfolio. Freddie Mac and Fannie Mae imposed foreclosure moratoriums. Repurchases. Mortgage Insurance rescissions. Jingle mail, when the homeowner sends in the keys. HAMP. HARP. Judicial foreclosures ground to a halt. Then the regulators and plaintiff attorneys came at you. Then the gift that keeps on giving: the CFPB. Maybe servicing isn't such a great idea. Several large banks significantly reduced holdings of servicing post-2010.

Stan Middleman sees disruption being thrust on the originator community by the owners of servicing:

> *"Not too many years ago our industry was dominated by the largest banks. Ninety percent of the servicing was in possession of the five largest banks. Today, that has certainly spread around and been diffused, and non-banks are as prevalent in the top 10 mortgage banks as banks are. Some of the changes that we see tend to put business in the hands of more entrepreneurial folks rather than institutional people and banks. I think that that will help them innovate, tactically, the approach to the consumer. ...Someday in the not horribly distant future, getting a loan will be much faster. The ability to get a loan much faster and much easier will lend consumers to be much more subject to the law of inertia and have a propensity to stay with the lender that they're with."*

Stan anticipates that holders of servicing can slash wait times and processing times as key drivers for consumers in a lender's servicing portfolio:

> *"If you could go to your computer, type in three lines, and all that information that you're required to have is already readily available to your lender and it takes two minutes, five minutes... I think you're going to tend to want to stay there."*

Stan has a broad view of the servicing asset as a source of revenue. Let's start with the question of, "How much scale is needed to make an economic return in servicing?"

Is large scale required for profitability in servicing? The answer is "not so much," *if* one has high-quality servicing from a credit perspective.

Servicing with low delinquency can be profitable without regard to scale, as the accompanying chart demonstrates. Can the lender afford the investment of cash into mortgage servicing rights? The question of servicing retention is one of operational strategy and cash flow. Surprisingly, servicing scale is not necessarily a driver of profitability.

Loan Servicing Economics

BASIS POINTS	<2,500	2,500 10,000	10,000 50,000	>50,000	Total
DIRECT REVENUE					
Servicing Fees	28.6	28.9	26.9	26.5	27.9
First Mortgages, Seconds, Other	28.6	26.8	25.9	20.8	26
Subservicing Fees Earned	-	2.2	1	5.7	1.9
Late Fees and Other Ancillary Income	1.3	2.4	2.3	3.7	2.3
Total Direct Servicing Revenue	**29.9**	**31.4**	**29.1**	**30.2**	**30.2**
DIRECT EXPENSES					
Personnel	7.1	4.6	3.4	9	5.1
Loan Administrative Employees	6.7	4.1	2.9	5	4.5
Benefits	0.3	0.4	0.4	0.9	0.5
Other Personnel Expense	0	0.2	0.1	0.2	0.1
Occupancy and Equipment	0.3	0.4	0.5	0.6	0.4
Other Direct Expenses	11.5	7.6	7.9	6.4	8.5
Subservicing Fees Paid	10.4	5.8	5.7	2	6.3
Other Miscellaneous Expenses	1.1	1.8	2.9	4.4	2.2
Total Direct Expenses	**18.8**	**12.7**	**11.7**	**12.9**	**14**
DIRECT SERVICING NET INCOME	**11.2**	**18.7**	**17.4**	**17.3**	**16.2**
INDIRECT EXPENSES					
Unreimbursed FC/REO Svg Expenses	-	0.5	0.3	1.9	0.5
Corporate Allocation	0.9	0.7	1.4	1.9	1.1
Total Indirect Expenses	**0.9**	**1.9**	**1.7**	**3.7**	**1.7**
NET INTEREST INCOME					
Escrow Earnings	0	0	0.1	0.8	0.2
Corporate Interest Losses on MBS Pools	-	-0.1	-0.2	-0.2	-0.1
Other Interest Expense	-0.1	-0.2	-0.5	-2.4	-0.6
Net Interest Income	**-0.1**	**-0.3**	**-0.5**	**-1.8**	**-0.6**
NET OPERATING INCOME	**10.1**	**17.3**	**15.2**	**11.7**	**14**

Source: MBA Mortgage Bankers Performance Report

JAMES M. DEITCH CPA, CMB

Does credit quality really control servicing profitability? Performing loan servicing is thought to be relatively easy. That may be true if ease of servicing is confined to collection of payments as set out above; however, servicing regulatory risk is very high and increasing, even for performing loans. Escrow analysis, satisfaction management, natural disaster impact, consumer confusion, and misunderstanding all contribute to regulatory risk.

Credit quality is just one dimension of servicing profitability.

CASH FLOW AND PROFITABILITY

Most lenders realize profit and cash flow are not equivalent. For example, Mortgage Servicing Rights ("MSRs") generate income when originated, but the cash flow is initially negative. Investment in "MSRs" is a use of cash. The investment yields a periodic flow of servicing fees, and some cash arising from escrow balances. Non-performing servicing can rapidly become a heavy use of cash, as investors require timely principal and interest payments, and taxes and insurance must be paid whether the borrower is current or delinquent. These requirements can adversely affect the cash flow and underlying liquidity[43] of a lender.

Generally accepted accounting principles ("GAAP") for mortgage banking can produce timing differences in profit versus cash flow. MSRs discussed previously are an example where income is recognized at the creation of the MSR, but the cash flow arising from servicing fees occurs over the life of the loan.

---

[43] http://www.wsfsledrangers.org/uploads/2/3/4/6/23466770/msr.pdf

The recognition of the fair value of locked loans may produce profit, but it does not generate immediate cash flow. Lenders that hedge secondary market transactions, as opposed to best efforts forward sales, can realize fair value profit from mark to market of the hedging derivatives. Publicly traded lenders contend with the SEC's Staff Accounting Bulletin 109 "Written Loan Commitments Recorded at Fair Value Through Earnings." This application of GAAP may generate timing differences between profit recognition and cash flow. Generally, these timing differences span less than 90 days, as they relate the origination and funding cycle of the underlying loans. We'll cover profit versus cash flow timing differences—short-term differences arising from the origination and funding cycle, and long-term differences related to servicing—a little later in this chapter.[44]

The basic equation, however, is that profit is the sole long-term source of capital growth and positive cash flow. Company, channel, region, and branch profitability are extremely important in managing a lender's business. A little secret—if an executive is a little defensive or self-conscious reading the last few paragraphs regarding profitability and cash-flow, they are not alone. There are many lenders, both IMBs *and* financial institutions, that have difficulty accurately and quickly reporting profit and cash flow to the company, channel, region, and branch level. I'll leave the details in the confessional but suffice it to say that profitability and cash flow reporting and forecasting are not the strong suits of many lenders. Martin Kerr of Loan Vision, Nathan Burch of Vellum, Jim MacLeod of Coastal States, and other Mavericks expressed amazement, as do I, at how otherwise sophisticated lenders have difficulties in these areas.

---

[44] https://www.sec.gov/interps/account/sab109.htm

LIQUIDITY AND YOUR BUSINESS STRATEGY

Cash flow and liquidity are the keys to successful mortgage banking. Without cash and liquidity, options and viability are severely reduced. What are the various cash cycles in mortgage banking? The monthly origination cash cycle, servicing cycle, Mortgage Servicing Rights cash cycle, default and foreclosure cash cycles? Pipeline growth and hedging cash cycles?

Mortgage Banking inherently consumes cash during the origination process. The chart below shows the hypothetical sources and uses of cash for a single loan originated via a retail channel with servicing retained, versus accrual profitability. This example is simplified and makes assumptions to illustrate the cash flow process. The amounts are in basis points:

Cash Flow Analysis of the Origination Process

DAYS FROM START OF CONSUMER INTEREST IN A LOAN	PHASE OF LOAN IN PROCESS	BASIS POINTS PER LOAN			
		REVENUE	COST	CUMULATIVE NET PRE-TAX PROFIT	CUMULATIVE NET CASH FLOW
0	CONSUMER INTEREST		20	-20	-20
10	LOAN APPLICATION	20		0	0
45	LOAN WORKFLOW MANAGEMENT		80	-80	-80
55	CONSUMER LOAN CLOSING		200	-280	-280
70	INVESTOR FUNDING	275	40	-45	-45
YEAR 1	CAPITALIZED MORTGAGE SERVICING RIGHTS	90		45	-45
	TOTAL	385	340	45	-45

The process starts with initial interest from a consumer. This initial interest could result from a purchased lead, a response to a website or social media, or a borrower identified by a loan officer. From initial consumer interest through application, about 20 basis points are expended for leads, marketing, credit reports, and associated costs of the infrastructure.

At loan application, the borrower is assumed to pay an application fee in addition to third-party fees, bringing the net cash back to neutral. This is assumed to occur on the 10th day after initial consumer interest.

Once the application is underway, labor for various operational activities and associated third-party costs are incurred, totaling about 80 basis points. If the loan falls out, the lender is cash negative for these costs incurred.

If the loan closes, loan officer, branch, and related compensation and costs are paid out on the 55th day. At this point, the lender is about 280 basis points cash negative. The lender then waits for loan funding by the investor, while paying shipping, post-closing, and any cure costs. At funding, the lender receives the purchase price and capitalizes the mortgage servicing asset, bringing the lender to a cash positive position of 45 basis points about 70 days after initial consumer interest.

When the lender is building a pipeline of loans, as in the Spring home-buying season or when interest rates fall, and refinance activity grows, the growth of the pipeline uses cash. When a lender's pipeline is falling, when home buying season is over, or rates increase reducing refinancing, the cash position of the lender improves. Note that cash flow and reported earnings are different.

In the discussion above, retained servicing means the lender will capitalize Mortgage Servicing Rights (MSRs) of 90 basis points and record the profit from capitalization. But the lender will not have the cash in hand. Rather, the capitalized MSRs will be financed out of the lender's capital. This requirement to finance MSRs is the issue Stan Middlemen described earlier where book profit and cash flow are not the same. The desire to retain MSRs consumes cash and requires capital to support the MSR, so a lender could be consuming cash and liquidity even while reporting book profit.

CHAPTER 7
STRATEGIC TRANSFORMATION APPLIED

Many executives I spoke with suggested that the book should include a chapter walking through the Strategic Transformation process. It seemed like a smart idea— after all, concrete examples make it easier to understand the Six Levers of Strategy and how they relate to the overall business. Looking at the past performance of a mortgage banker and forward to the expected, transformed performance of the same company would provide a context for where a company has been, where it is now, and where it's going in relation to Strategic Transformation.

Thank you for the suggestion, everyone. Let's apply it to a company I'll call NewMortgage Company. This company is a composite created using actual data from a number of mortgage banking enterprises. The data is anonymized, but the thrust of the Strategic Transformation accurately represents the strategies employed by the composite entities. It also accurately represents the fictional NewMortgage Company's transformation to a company that provides outstanding customer service, defect-free loans, and superior profitability.

The chart below shows the past financial performance of NewMortgage over the past three years. The 'past' column is the average of three years of data. The 'present' is the most recent nine months of operations. The 'future' is the desired operational results of the transformed NewMortgage Company.

	PAST		PRESENT YTD		FUTURE STATE	
	DOLLARS	BASIS POINTS	DOLLARS	BASIS POINTS	DOLLARS	BASIS POINTS
Loans Closed	1,700,000,000		1,331,000,000		1,250,000,000	
Average Loan Size	349,000.00		331,000.00		247,000.00	
Gain on Sale	51,340,000	3.02%	38,255,700	2.87%	49,500,000	3.96%
Sales Compensation	29,400,000	1.73%	24,300,000	1.83%	24,750,000	1.98%
Other Compensation	14,000,000	0.82%	11,156,000	0.84%	13,400,000	1.07%
Other Expenses	6,320,000	0.37%	4,300,000	0.32%	3,750,000	0.30%
Pretax Profit	**1,620,000**	**0.10%**	**(1,500,300)**	**-0.11%**	**7,600,000**	**0.61%**

Note that the average of the last three years of pretax profit averaged about 10 basis points. The current year-to-date shows signs of margin compression resulting in a loss in the 9 or so months year to date.

This lender's current strategic map shows attempted use of economies of scale to compete, with an element of technology sprinkled in as point solutions to specific, perceived problems. Many of the technology point solutions, however, are used to foster recruiting and retention by permitting loan officers to 'have it my way.' In essence, the loan officers run the company. The result of loan officer control is that loan officers and producing branch managers make on average twelve times more per loan than NewMortgage does. The current strategy leads to volume without profit and the need for Strategic Transformation.

A DEEP DIVE ON NEWMORTGAGE

Let's deconstruct the historical operations of the retail channel of NewMortgage to gain some better insight. We'll stick to retail for simplicity; we could look at the wholesale and correspondent channels in the same way. Here are the key metrics for the year-to-date results:

UNITS	VOLUME ($MILLIONS)	AVERAGE LOAN SIZE	TIME TO CLOSE	TIME TO INVESTOR FUNDING	REVENUE	REVENUE (BPS)
3,798	1,331	$350,360	42	60	$38,255,700	287

The screen below is using Coheus™, which according to Nathan Burch of Vellum Mortgage, provides actionable profit intelligence to lenders. We'll use Coheus to explore the year to date results for each branch's turnaround time, loan officer performance, and the credit box down to the loan level. The credit box includes FICO scores, loan to value, and debt to income. Turnaround looks at how long it takes for each loan to proceed through each milestone of application taken through investor funding.

A LOOK AT LOAN PRODUCTION METRICS

For now, we'll only look at closed loans. Later, we'll do the same for the pipeline. Here's the screen.

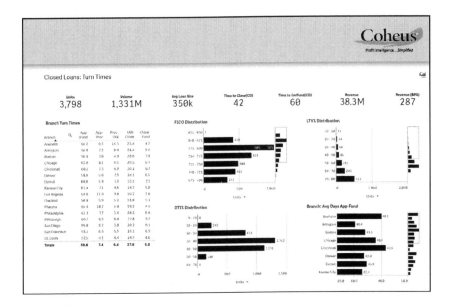

A couple of factors jump out. The FICO scores represent a very high credit quality cohort of borrowers with a relatively low gain on sale revenue and a high average loan balance. Conventional lending is likely the focus of NewMortgage.

The next thing we have to explore are the margins of the branches. The overall NewMortgage margin is 287 basis points. The view below excludes one branch, St. Louis, and the result is that the NewMortgage margin jumps to 347 basis points, excluding the $255 million volume of St. Louis.

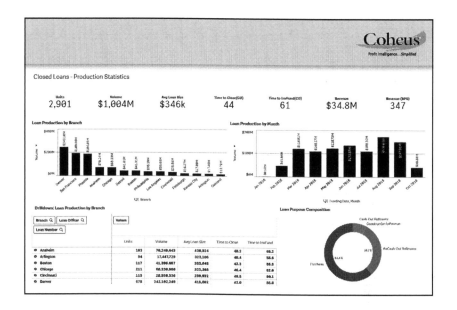

A DEEPER LOOK AT A PROBLEM BRANCH

So, what is happening in St. Louis? Lots of volume, but little margin.

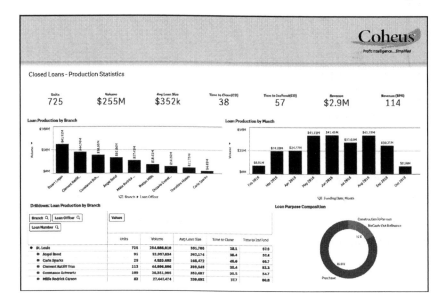

With 114 basis points as the average, what about the various credit box elements? Let's look at FICO between 600 and 700, LTVs between 80 and 100, and DTIs over 40. This would be the lower end of the credit box for most lenders. Surprisingly, the margin on these loans was 88 basis points on the $22 million of closing in this cohort, as set out below.

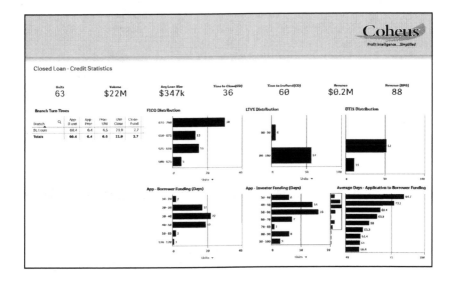

The margin on the higher credit score loans over 700 was 142 basis points. Something's not adding up here.

LOAN OFFICER METRICS

Let's look at the individual loan officer results. Six loan officers focusing on purchase business produced $111 million of loans at 268 basis points of margin. Not great, but more than twice the margin of the branch as a whole.

JAMES M. DEITCH CPA, CMB

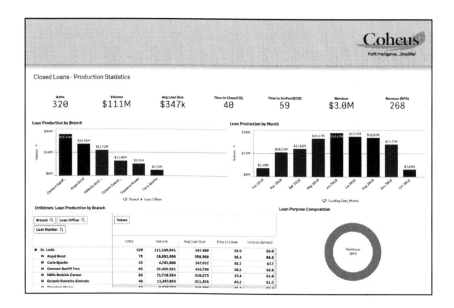

Loan officer Constance Schwartz did $39 million of volume at negative 60 basis points of margin. Stuart Logan and Ms. Schwartz combined for $100 million of loan closings, at negative 32 basis points of gross margin, as set out below.

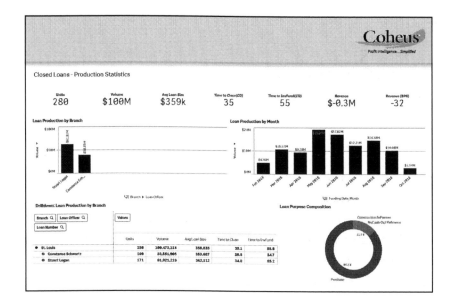

Next, what is the quality of these loans? The quality assurance reviews of St. Louis are favorable. Of the 134 loans reviewed, only 6 loans had defects, and only 2 loans had critical defects. Poor profit margins, but credit quality and QC results are okay.

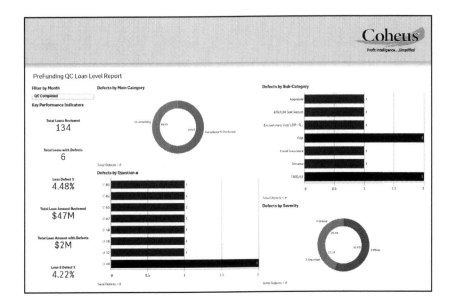

The issue at hand with St. Louis is high balance conventional lending. The branch has a very high purchase business, but much of it is high balance. The issue was further exasperated by a marketing services agreement with a real estate agency where much of the volume came from. This is a living example of the adverse impact of the volume that a few high producing loan officers can have. It looked good on paper— $100 million of purchase business from two producers.

The purchase component of the year to date closings overall have the following metrics, with the margin about 75 basis points better than the overall average.

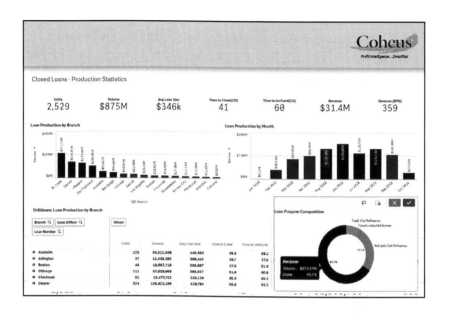

The refinance mix is another story, with gross margins of 131 basis points on $361 million of volume. You may ask why even do refinance business at 131 basis points? It's probably not covering loan originator commissions. Great question.

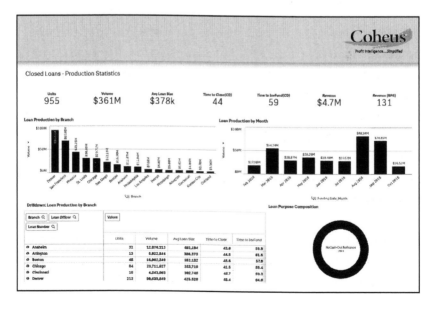

Phoenix, St. Louis, Anaheim, Philadelphia, and three other branches have even worse refinance margins of 63 basis points.

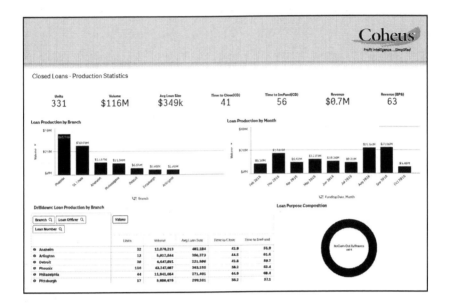

NewMortgage will need to carefully look at the Economies of Scale and Product Niche levers because the origination model is not being optimized. It's made much worse by Dodd-Frank commission regulations which prohibit paying different commissions on purchase and refinance business as they are loan terms. As a result, the loan officers bring a high percentage of purchase business, but the offset is that their commission rates for purchase producers mean the refinance business is at best breakeven. There's a lot more going on here, and we'll jump into that below.

This is not just a St. Louis problem, it's across all of the branches. The lowest performing loan officers are not just in one branch. If we looked at the 12 lowest performing loan officers, the compensation

JAMES M. DEITCH CPA, CMB

cost was 1,436 basis points and the loans they closed lost 1,048 basis points. The 28 loans for $5.4 million in principal balance cost the company about $600,000 in direct sales compensation. That's before the costs of fulfillment personnel, sales management, other direct costs etc. In other words, this team of low performers hidden among 7 branches cost NewMortgage about $1 million of pretax profit. Recall that NewMortgage lost about $1.5 million year to date, and we just identified the 12 loan officers responsible for the bulk of the losses with $5.4 million of production.

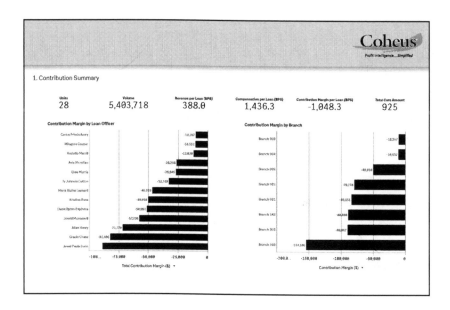

This is why the NewMortgage Economies of Scale lever is working in reverse. The strategy of "all production is good production" produces significant losses in the effort to grow the production base to cover overhead. A better solution for NewMortgage is the surgical removal of all loan originators below the cut line. Billy Beane summed it up for me: "They're professionals. Just tell them they've been traded or sent to the minors."

OPERATIONAL ELEMENTS

Let's take a look at the use of Technology and Process Transformation at NewMortgage, specifically Time to Close of 42 days and Time to Investor Funding of 60 days. Time to Close is average, but 18 days to investor funding indicates some issues for review.

Units	Volume $millions	Avg Loan Size	Time to Close	Time to Investor Funding	Revenue	Revenue (BPS)
3,798	1,331	350,360	42	60	38,254,970	287

The first question is to look at the impact of the credit box on Time to Close. One would expect high FICO, low LTV loans would be 'slam dunks', proceeding quickly through NewMortgage. Not quite, as loans with FICOs over 700 and LTVs under 70 take longer to close and fund, 47 and 63 days respectively, and these loans have margins of 105 basis points in total.

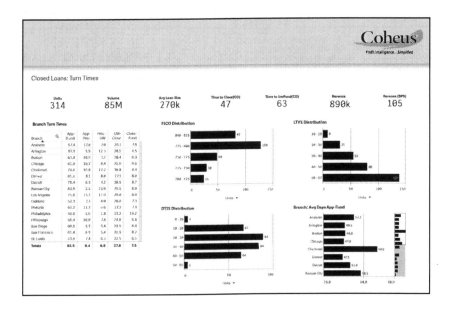

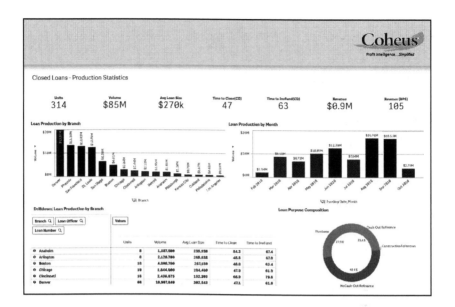

The Application to Consumer Loan Closing takes an average of 42 days. The distribution analysis below shows that the average is 42 days, the median is 38 days, and the standard deviation is 21 days. The shape of the curve shows that a significant number of loan closings extend beyond 45 days. Recall that consumer satisfaction is heavily based on the speed of transaction. The longer times to close can lead to poorly perceived customer service. We can also see the variation in closing times among the branches.

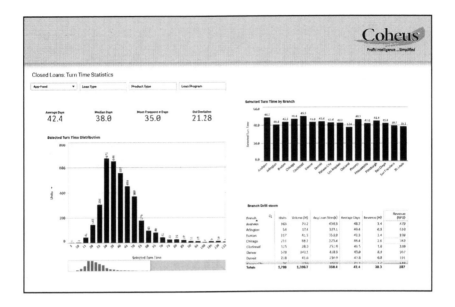

The worst performing three branches with turnaround times over 50 days are Anaheim, Philadelphia, and Phoenix. The branches account for 192 loans that took an average of 85 days to close. Interestingly, these loans produced gross margins of 389 basis points.

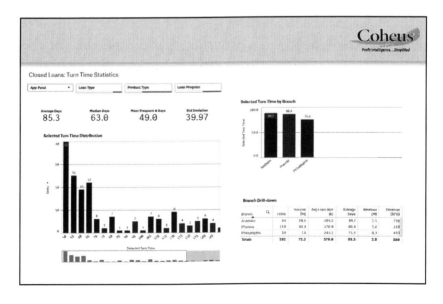

JAMES M. DEITCH CPA, CMB

The credit box of these 192 loans was pretty strong; nonetheless, these loans spent 20 days getting from application to processing and 49 days in underwriting.

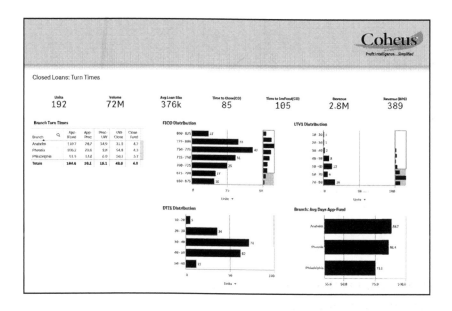

Further analysis indicates there is a wide variation among the employees involved in these loans. Loans taking over 100 days are concentrated in loan originator Dominique Ashley. Processing on average took 15 days, but Riley Weeks averaged 35 days. Underwriting took 49 days on average, but Nettie Burns took 70 days on 23 loans.

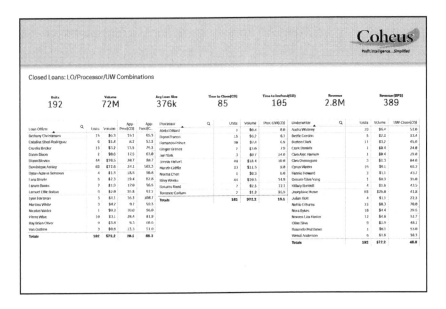

Looking just at Dominique Ashley, her loans spent 9 days in processing but an average of 69 days in underwriting. Dominique's gross margin on these loans was 259 basis points, well below the average for purchase business, and these loans were 25 VA loans, 20 conventional, and 18 FHA loans.

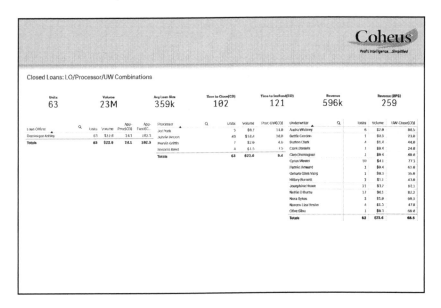

Switch to the pipeline for Dominique, she has 37 loans in the pipeline, about half of which are not locked. Most of hers are being processed by Johnnie Herbert. 19 loans are approved, but not closed.

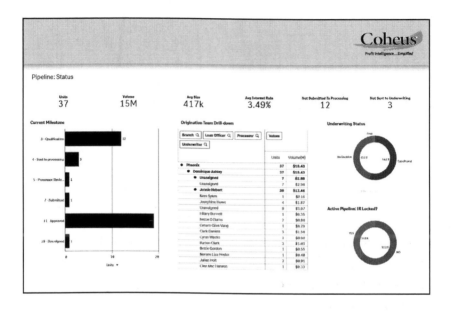

Next, let's examine underwriting turnaround times in more detail. There are significant variations in underwriting times, from a low of 14 days to a high of 50 days. Here's the chart of turnaround performance.

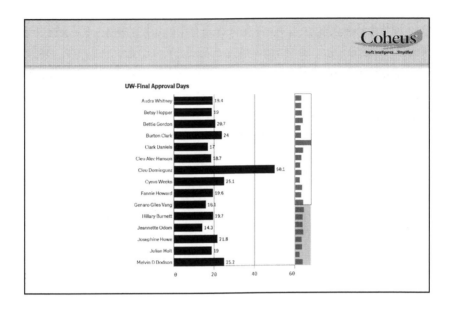

Aside from customer service levels, long periods in underwriting usually mean lots of underwriting touches, which inevitably increases the likelihood of underwriting errors. Here is an extract of the throughput of five underwriters and the cost per decision, together with their respective quality assurance findings. One could analyze underwriters, processors, closers, and shippers in the same manner.

UNDERWRITER	TURN-AROUND TIME	SALARY, INCENTIVES AND BENEFITS	MONTHLY COST	FILES DECISIONED PER MONTH	COST PER FILE DECISIONED	QC CRITICAL DEFECT FINDINGS RATE
Cleo Dominguez	50	77,000	6,417	29	221	19%
Cyrus Weeks	25	88,000	7,333	39	188	12%
Josephine Howe	22	95,000	7,917	52	152	8%
Betsy Hopper	19	73,000	6,083	42	145	3%
Tracey Cooley	14	86,000	7,167	51	141	9%

Cure costs are another area where profit is lost. There are a variety of reasons that require cures, but the end result is that NewMortgage is shredding hundred dollar bills in the paper shredder. Cure costs are usually unforced errors. A root cause of cure costs identified fee tolerance issues as the largest element of cure costs. These cures are truly unforced errors, arising from systemic failure.

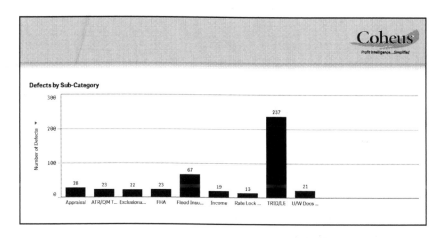

STRATEGIC TRANSFORMATION OF NEWMORTGAGE

NewMortgage is unprofitable for a variety of reasons. One could use the 'whack a mole' strategy and implement point solutions for the company. Perhaps a mobile app would help retail loan officers work better with customers. A couple of workflow management tools may improve throughput. A business intelligence tool could look at loan production statistics. Ad hoc exception reporting could be utilized. These are all valuable tools.

In fact, NewMortgage *had* implemented all of these point solution tools, provided by a variety of vendors.

New Mortgage was still unprofitable despite the efforts of the management team. The various point solutions and attempts at correcting process and originator matters were overshadowed by the quest for volume to cover overhead extending from the singular focus on Economies of Scale. Point solutions will not solve NewMortgage's myriad of issues. NewMortgage's primary strategic lever of Economies of Scale wasn't working.

However, the CEO decided to conduct a Strategic Transformation to set the future state of the business. After considerable discussion, NewMortgage would make heavy use of the Product Niche, Relationship and Empathy, and Technology and Process Transformation strategic levers as set forth below.

The Product Niche lever will be adjusted to focus on loan officers that produce a targeted and consistent loan volume where loan quality can be processed and underwritten according to the company's service standards. The targeted niches will be government and non-QM lending in second-tier markets, as opposed to first tier markets such as the 20 major metro areas in the U.S.

The Relationship and Empathy lever will complement the Product Niche lever, serving market segments that value face-to-face relationships, recruiting loan officers that excel at working with borrowers, structuring loans that suit a borrower's circumstances, and working with realtors and builders that serve these customer market segments.

The Technology and Process Transformation will start with a governance model that puts daily performance metrics for every employee transparently in front of the employee, the employee's peers, the employee's management team, and executive management. The business process will be transformed, starting with the end in mind: outstanding customer service, defect-free loans, and a pretax margin of at least 60 basis points. NewMortgage committed to configure its existing LOS and other tools to complement the Product Niche and Relationship/Empathy levers.

The decision to continue with the existing LOS was made largely because the issues with process and efficiency were not LOS driven. NewMortgage had implemented the LOS about six years previously, pre TRID, and used the 'out of the box' configuration initially, with many point solution 'tweaks' in the ensuing six years. NewMortgage never conducted a post-implementation 'back to front-end' review.

STRATEGIC LEVERS AND EXPECTED RESULTS

The Product Niche lever will be adjusted to focus more on FHA, VA, and non-QM products. This means a change in geographic focus as well as the change in the skill sets of loan officers employed. Conventional lending will still be offered, but NewMortgage will simply eliminate unprofitable volume by terminating any loan officers below the NewMortgage loan profitability cut line. These actions will make a significant increase in overall margin, as follows:

PRODUCT	MARGIN TARGET	LOAN VOLUME ($)	GROSS MARGIN TARGET ($)
Conventional	3.00%	600,000,000	18,000,000
FHA/VA	5.50%	400,000,000	22,000,000
Non-QM	4.25%	200,000,000	8,500,000
Jumbo	2.00%	50,000,000	1,000,000
Total	3.96%	1,250,000,000	49,500,000

The future state of NewMortgage will be as follows:

	PAST		PRESENT YTD		FUTURE STATE	
	DOLLARS	BASIS POINTS	DOLLARS	BASIS POINTS	DOLLARS	BASIS POINTS
Loans Closed	1,700,000,000		1,331,000,000		1,250,000,000	
Average Loan Size	349,000.00		331,000.00		247,000.00	
Gain on Sale	51,340,000	3.02%	38,255,700	2.87%	49,500,000	3.96%
Sales Compensation	29,400,000	1.73%	24,300,000	1.83%	24,750,000	1.98%
Other Compensation	14,000,000	0.82%	11,156,000	0.84%	13,400,000	1.07%
Other Expenses	6,320,000	0.37%	4,300,000	0.32%	3,750,000	0.30%
Pretax Profit	**1,620,000**	**0.10%**	**(1,500,300)**	**-0.11%**	**7,600,000**	**0.61%**

The Strategic Transformation was achieved by:

- Working with the executive team and senior managers to adopt the Strategic Transformation vision of NewMortgage, which included terminating a few executives who refused to buy in to the vision.
- Quickly reconfiguring the LOS to support the Strategic Lever Map of NewMortgage.
- Recruiting a team that had significant government lending experience.
- Recruiting a team that focused on non-QM products.
- Adding the non-QM investors.
- Cutting loan officers and operational employees that refused to adopt the vision and whose performance was below the loan profitability cut line. The cuts were made in sequence, starting with loan officers whose production was far below the cut line.
- The first round of loan officers and operational personnel cuts actually provided a significant boost to NewMortgage's

profitability. This was because the cuts of loan officers and fulfillment personnel were made simultaneously, and the remaining loan production was re-allocated to the most efficient processors and underwriters.

- Executives spent lots of face time with the remaining team and in welcoming and integrating the new team members. Interestingly, the reaction of the remaining original New-Mortgage team members was, "What took you so long to make these changes?"

The following are the results of the Strategic Transformation. The product margins for the new branches are as follows:

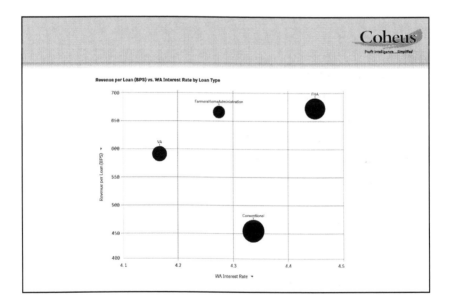

MEASURING LOAN LEVEL PROFITABILITY

The most profitable loan officers and branches are achieving 530 basis points of gross margin, at a loan officer compensation cost of 128 basis points. This yields over 400 basis points in net contribution margin after loan officer sales compensation. $166 million of loan production is providing $6.6 million in contribution margin to NewMortgage. Recall the two loan officers in St. Louis that produced $100 million and lost $1 million in net contribution margin for NewMortgage. The swap of those two loan officers with the $90 million of new production from recruited branches resulted in a $7.6 million positive profit swing for NewMortgage.

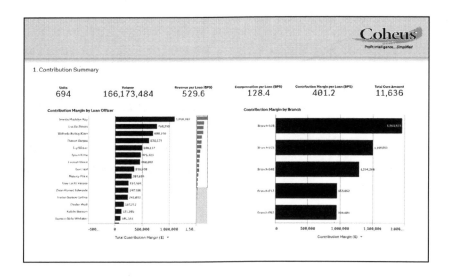

The overall results are tracking well for NewMortgage. The targeted margin of 396 basis points is being achieved. Recruiting costs, signing bonuses, and termination costs of loan officers below the cut line are increasing total compensation costs, including branch manager compensation, to 257 basis points, but there are transition-related costs that will ultimately see sales compensation moving to the target of 198 basis points for the year.

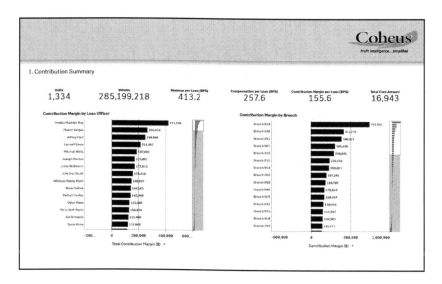

NewMortgage instituted a robust prefunding quality assurance function to increase the number of defect-free loans. Increased transparency comes from sharing the prefunding results with team members and tracking error rates among NewMortgage employee roles.

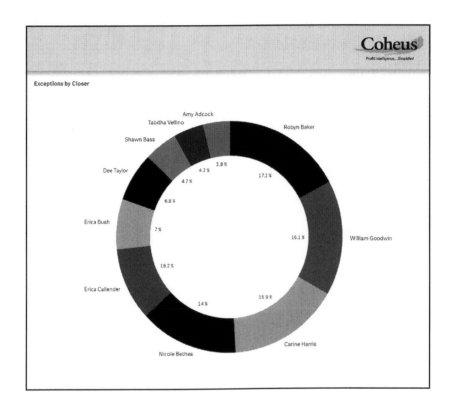

NewMortgage also set the following calendar day operational targets for the fulfillment team:

MILESTONE	MINIMUM SERVICE LEVEL	TARGET SERVICE LEVEL
Application to Processing	3	1
Processing to Underwriting	10	6
Underwriting to Clear to Close	10	7
CTC to Closing	15	12
Closing to Funding	7	5
Total Cycle Time	**45**	**31**

Speed through the warehouse is being monitored. The dwell on the warehouse is down to 14 days from the 21 days year to date:

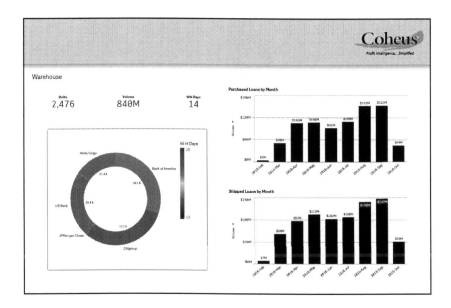

NewMortgage is monitoring these service levels with a master scheduler and a clock solution for transparency to each member of the NewMortgage sales, operational, and managerial teams. Finally, NewMortgage has set a 98% customer satisfaction rate. Dissatisfied customers receive a call from a senior executive offering to resolve any issue to the satisfaction of the customer. This personal outreach to customers increases the bond between customers and NewMortgage. It's producing more referral business and is a positive influence on new loan officer and branch acquisition.

NewMortgage is well on its way to outstanding customer service, defect-free loans, and an acceptable profit margin in a tough market.

CONCLUSION

A plan of action to achieve three simultaneous goals: superior profitability, outstanding customer satisfaction, and defect-free loans.

That is strategy, and that is what I hope you take away from this book. We've discussed the power of the six strategic levers those in the mortgage banking industry can use to implement high-level, game-changing strategy.

As you move forward in your work, revisit these ideas and consider how they can activate Strategic Transformation in our industry:

1. Expanding to achieve **economies of scale.**

2. Adjusting **channels of distribution.**

3. Becoming **technologically and process transformative.**

4. Exploiting **product niche or niches.**

5. **Diversifying** beyond consumer mortgage banking.

6. Increasing the level of **relationship and empathy** when interacting with prospects and customers.

Of equal importance, consider which of these levers will be your focus.

We've also discussed how tactical decisions and old ways of doing things do not comprise an effective approach and do not lead to Strategic Transformation. Thought leaders in the industry need to shift paradigms and start thinking about a future of mortgage banking that steps away from entrenched patterns of the past.

Clayton Christensen put it well: "The reason why it is so difficult for existing firms to capitalize on disruptive innovations is that their processes and their business models that make them good at the existing business actually make them bad at competing for the disruptive transformation."

What has been in place for the mortgage banking industry both since the Crisis and since the Depression is holding us back. The very things that have kept us feeling secure until now are the issues that will keep us from responding effectively to disruption. If anything, I hope this book opens up a conversation amongst thought leaders in the industry, and that we can start discussing how we can leverage disruptive innovations. Certainly, our traditional approach has been sufficient until now— but we cannot afford, as an industry, to miss out on or mistake the next big shift.

Remember Peter in "Moneyball"? He told us all we need to hear: "There's an epidemic failure within the game to understand what's really happening... they're asking the wrong questions." As an industry, we need to start asking the right questions.

- How are demographic shifts redefining what customers expect for residential finance?
- How will the substantial increase in homeowners' equity shift the role mortgage bankers play in residential finance?
- How can mortgage bankers diversify into related markets, such as homeowner's insurance, and achieve overall financial management goals?
- How can new products that serve millennials, minorities, and customers with non-traditional employment be safely developed?
- How will the human needs of relationship and empathy be conveyed to borrowers by mortgage bankers? How can technology enhance that relationship and empathy?

- How can we get the cost of originating purchase mortgage to $1,000?
- How can we get credit decisions to the speed of a credit card decision?

And hundreds of others.

The mortgage industry needs to rethink how we get wins. That may mean relearning what it means to get a run, how to value assets and embracing Strategic Transformation.

CHAPTER 8
INFORMATION SECURITY FOR MAVERICKS

First, my thanks to Mauricio Valverde, a Teraverde associate and recent Penn State graduate who substantially contributed to this chapter.

Strategic Lever 3 is Technological and Process Transformation. It's no secret that Mavericks consider the information security element of Technological and Process Transformation as a major priority when it comes to protecting their business resources and client data. As technology and its inherent threats continue to develop at an unprecedented speed, we are reaching an era in which the true Mavericks must keep up with the latest in FinTech while also delivering the heightened information security both companies and their customers need.

Knowing where to begin isn't easy. As Brian Stoffers, Chairman of the MBA mentioned in the article *Stoffers: Industry Faces 'Enormous Strategic Decisions' to Shape Future*, "Many MBA members struggle with how to take the first step or in what direction. Additionally, many don't have the financial resources larger companies have. Nonetheless, the noted MBA and industry leaders have been urging its members to invest in technology or run the risk of becoming obsolete."[45]

One very salient point Stoffers raises is that technology policy can differ drastically from state to state, creating roadblocks and confusion for FinTech companies. In response, Stoffers writes, the MBA is stepping in, attempting to establish a single technology infrastructure for all states and encouraging state and federal regulators to resist the urge to revise cybersecurity requirements on a state by state basis. This would allow businesses to explore and implement technology to improve their business without unnecessary roadblocks.

So, there's some good news in all this.

But the stakes are high in an industry like mortgage banking where so much non-public consumer information is on the line. Any mortgage loan application contains a complete financial snapshot of the borrower— income, assets, credit lines, loans, employment information, social security numbers, work history — making the industry a target for bad actors. Developing new technologies while still protecting the consumer is critical for the industry and society at large, for that matter— after all, the financial services industry has been designated as one of the six critical infrastructure sectors in the United States.

REQUIRED REGULATORY SAFEGUARDS

The "safeguards" rule of the Gramm Leach Bliley Act (GLBA), which applies to banks and mortgage bankers, calls for lenders to utilize the best security approach that is both readily available

---

[45] https://www.mba.org/cmf-newslinks/2018/april/mba-cmf-newslink-4-19-18/stoffers-industry-faces-enormous-strategic-decisions-to-shape-future

and cost-effective. Information Security is often considered the purview of the IT Department, but in practice, it should be one of the key priorities of the Maverick CEO. Information Security is not just about firewalls and technical systems; security is a business strategy that must be embedded throughout the mortgage banking operation. With more solutions streaming into mortgage banking from FinTech, there are more opportunities to have data lost or misappropriated.

A number of peer to peer payment applications emerged in recent years to challenge commercial banks' domination of the payment markets. These peer to peer services move far beyond the bill pay and ATM payment technologies. One company, Venmo[46], used Strategic Lever 3 to substantially innovate the peer to peer payment application space.

The Venmo application is a peer to peer cash transfer mobile application. A PayPal owned app, Venmo creates a user-friendly way to receive and transfer money to others. A user can create an account connected to their bank account or credit card. Tech-savvy users are adapting to this new way of managing their transactions. The use of the app is almost ubiquitous now, coming into play in daily life, as when a group of friends go to a bar and then have to pay the bill. Multiple friends can transfer money in an instant to one friend, allowing a single person to pay for the bill.

According to my millennial Teraverde associate Mauricio Valverde, *"Venmo makes splitting a bill at a restaurant simple and easy when I'm with my friends."* The transfer to their bank account doesn't post immediately, however. That's because Venmo examines the payment transaction and checks for fraud, insufficient funds, or

---

[46] Venmo was acquired in 2012 by Braintree; PayPal acquired Braintree and Venmo in 2013.

other problems, understanding the absolute necessity for security in FinTech.

The intersection of cash balances, social media, and electronic communication opens reputational, legal, and economic risks to companies. Venmo encountered regulatory difficulties in this, which is not unusual for a FinTech company. The intricacies of financial services consumer disclosure were not totally understood. Venmo didn't explicitly disclose that funds could be frozen or removed from a user's account in certain circumstances, for example. Additionally, Venmo claimed their app had embedded "bank-grade security systems." Venmo's data security violated the GLB Privacy Rule 'by failing to have a written information security program in place before August 2014 and by failing to implement safeguards to protect the security, confidentiality, and integrity of consumer data until at least March 2015.' The user's information is displayed in newsfeeds which any person, with or without an account, can access to view past transactions.[47]

SECURITY THREATS IN THE MORTGAGE PROCESS

Down payments are essential elements to mortgage closings. Funds transfers, whether by Venmo, traditional bank wire transfers, or other methods, are often targets of scammers— a fact that has serious implications in mortgage banking. Over the past two years, one recurring act of fraud is the theft of a consumer's down payment for a mortgage.

---

[47] https://www.ftc.gov/news-events/blogs/business-blog/2018/02/venmo-settlement-addresses-availability-funds-privacy

The scam works like this, according to a Bulletin issued by N Caride, Acting Commissioner of the State of New Jersey De‍ ment of Banking:

> *"The purpose of this Bulletin is to remind you of the prevalence of fraudulent schemes to divert funds transferred by wire. These scams generally involve several types of business email compromise ("BEC") techniques that alter normal wiring instructions to divert funds from the intended recipient to a stranger.*
>
> *BEC schemes may use social engineering or computer intrusion techniques, such as malware and phishing. With sophisticated hacking mechanisms, a perpetrator will target weakly guarded transactions and, for instance, send the buyer an email from an address nearly identical to the closing agent's, with a plausible subject line, advising of a "wiring change."[48]*
>
> *When the buyer complies, the funds are wired to a scammer who is often overseas and usually impossible to track down. One precaution law enforcement agencies have urged is a "call and verify" routine, but scammers are now deploying phone "porting" technologies, to intrude into that safeguarding process, masquerading as a trusted party.*
>
> *There are innumerable versions of wire fraud, but they share one unfortunate result: the diverted funds are very difficult, if not impossible, to recover."*

Unfortunately, many CEOs have confided that their companies have been scammed by business email compromise and variants

---

[48] https://www.state.nj.us/dobi/bulletins/blt18_04.pdf

thereof. The losses range from a few thousand dollars to hundreds of thousands of dollars per incident. Reputational risk, legal wrangling, and confusion only add to the financial losses in these scenarios.

Mavericks do have options to protect against these types of security breaches. It is extraordinarily inexpensive to continuously train your workforce using a tool like KnowB4 or similar social engineering training/testing services. I highly recommend this type of safeguard.

Those in the mortgage banking industry also need to watch over the social space in addition to monitoring consumer data and employee behaviors. More and more frequently, financial institutions and lenders are engaging with the consumer through social media platforms such as Facebook, LinkedIn, Instagram, Twitter etc. More importantly, employees of banks and lenders frequently post content. The line between corporate and personal posts is often blurred.

Any content posted that is associated with a company needs to be evaluated across multiple criteria, including but not limited to where it is being posted and whether it is suitable for your ideal customer. Institutions and companies should interact with their audience by delivering educational articles, webinars, industry updates, downloadable books, and interactive campaigns, but should keep in mind that their brand is an extension of their digital image.

You cannot sidestep this type of engagement at this point. Building a digital image is vital for any business looking to increase engagement and relationships with their audience. Not having a social media presence, in fact, can make a company almost irrelevant in this day and age. The downside of social engagement, of course, is that it can provide hackers with more ways in. From fraudulent social media pages to malware posing as your company's content; engagement in the online world carries its risks. One click is all it takes. Make sure that your company is mitigating security risks by outsourcing, monitoring, and preventing these issues to third-party security providers.

Strategic Lever 3 is a necessary part of Strategic Transformation. As mentioned in Chapter 3, Quicken Rocket Mortgage became the backbone of Quicken's success story.

Even traditional face to face mortgage activities quickly move to the electronic domain. As mentioned by Gene Lugat of PrimeLending:

> *"Over 90 percent of borrowers choose their primary source of communication [as] text."*

Consumers are using their mobile devices more than *any other device* when engaging in banking and financial management activity. Just as a consumer can monitor bank transactions or financial activity via an app, mortgage consumers expect to access and monitor every step of the mortgage process via their mobile devices. Pizza Hut or Domino's delivery models provide apps that track your pizza from the moment you place your order until it arrives at your house. If Pizza Hut and Dominos can do it for pizza, why is it so hard to do it for a mortgage transaction?

What does the mortgage industry need to do to keep up? As Gene Lugat from PrimeLending put it:

> *"The consumer is taking the industry [towards strategic transformation] ... what does that mean for the current structure and architecture of our industry? What do we look like or what do we need to look like to meet and mirror the needs of a changing demographic shift in our industry that we're seeing today across the country?"*

As more technology is adopted, the need for new ways of verifying information arises. How will the mortgage banking industry use voice recognition or face verification to mitigate security breaches?

It's not just in banking— many other industries are also picking up on the consumer's tech preference. Millennials are shaping the way companies deliver service. For those concerned about how tech will affect consumer touch, it's important to keep in mind that these consumers are more self-reliant and *prefer* the most efficient and economical service for their product. In other words, they view enhanced tech as *enhanced customer service*. They expect security as a built-in and convenient component of every application.

Ross Diedrich from Covered Insurance Solutions is driving transformation in the homeowners' insurance industry by disintermediating traditional insurance agents.

> *"A recent study by the insurance institute came out and said there has been a 20 percent decrease year over year in customers who want to use a local agent. It's about 52 percent of consumers actually buy insurance because of a relationship and that trend is looking like it will be closer to 30 percent over the next couple of years. People no longer care about that face to face relationship and they instead want a fast and efficient and easy experience online."*

The homeowners' insurance area has competitors, such as Covered and Matic Insurance Services, transforming one of the hassles of owning a home: homeowners' insurance. Both companies work with originators and servicers to quickly obtain insurance quotes for homeowners engaged in obtaining a mortgage or renewing insurance for their loan servicer.

Making insurance shopping comparisons easy and accurate requires the exchange of data about the homeowner and the property to produce a quote that can be found online. Complications for information security arise, as more convenience and accuracy for the consumer requires a richer dataset to be exchanged.

The amount of diligence and ongoing vendor management of the partners in a mortgage banking transaction escalate quickly. Jonathan Corr of Ellie Mae stated,

> *"Encompass is a platform that enables the secure exchange of large amounts of data among customers, lenders, and lender partners. The security needs for securing data are immense."*

Selim Aissi, Chief Information Security Officer (CISO) at Ellie Mae shared the following insights:

> *"Ellie Mae invests much time and money in information security. Effective security needs to be built in, not added on. Every CEO in the industry needs to have security top of mind. "Social Engineering Threats."*

According to Mr. Aissi, executives need to work constantly on efforts to prevent data breaches. "Social engineering is one of the major attack vectors for security breaches. Social engineering constantly evolves, and education is a major element of risk mitigation."

Employees need training to ensure that they understand the nature of phishing attacks. This is one key factor in any security plan. According to the KnowBe4 website, '91% of data breaches started with a spear phishing attack.'

As an example: Two years ago, KnowBe4 experts received a request from a school that had been hit with a cyber-attack. When the team examined the school's system, they found the school was attacked on *a weekly basis*, in fact, and that it had been the target of a DDoS attack lasting *for 2 months*[49]. The company quickly implemented security protocols and started training staff to recognize and avoid phishing emails. Random testing of the staff showed a 27% click rate on phishing emails at first; five months later the clicks dropped to less than 1% ensuring a much more secure work environment.

Sometimes, threats will show up on your doorstep with a friendly face. One security group was hired by a Midwest power company to go undercover and identify all the ways they were prone to a cyber-attack. The security team sent some of their employees into the company disguised as service providers to check on speed issues the company was having with the internet. The fake "service providers" were graciously given a pass to go into the internet server, until a manager asked them for identification. After that attempt, it didn't get any better. The security team returned, this time after hours. They easily entered the building by picking a lock and left thumb drives on tables and even hooked up malware into the central system.[50]

Mortgage bankers deploy branches and loan officers to remote locations. The Loan Origination System is a treasure trove of Personally Identifiable Information (PII), including credit reports, social security numbers, employment histories, and lists of assets—everything a criminal could want. In some cases, even ethically impaired loan officers or branch managers might also want it.

---

[49] https://www.knowbe4.com/hubfs/Education.pdf

[50] https://www.businessinsider.com/hackers-power-grid-company-redteam-video-2016-9

Most LOS systems are provided as Software as a Service (SaaS), meaning the LOS provider hosts the system and provides overall system security. The lender's system administrator maintains access controls but oftentimes permits excessive system privileges due to poorly defined LOS roles and responsibilities. Excessive user privileges are often at the heart of PII loss from LOS systems.

LITIGATION RISK

PII loss can have significant consequences. According to Housing Wire, "A California jury ordered Guaranteed Rate to pay more than $25 million in damages to a fellow mortgage lender, Mount Olympus Mortgage Company, stemming from accusations that a former employee of Mount Olympus Mortgage stole client information and loan files and took them with him when he went to work at Guaranteed Rate."

Frequent litigation arises from allegedly inadequate controls over a lender's pipeline of leads and loans. The litigation often occurs when employees from a branch office resign, and the lender losing the branch performs a forensic review and discovers that some of their data was removed in the process. This happens often enough that informed thought leaders in the industry have to find ways to protect themselves and their customers.

In another instance, a lender belatedly found out that a just hired top loan officer transferred the entire contents, several gigabytes, of her former employer's laptop to the new lender. This included PII and other proprietary information of the former lender. The lender intervened, destroyed the data, and severely admonished the new loan officer and the low-level IT employee that unwittingly helped the loan officer. The lender then never fully trusted the loan officer, and the relationship didn't last long.

Considering these incidents, Mavericks know Information Security does not just include technical systems. It's the procedures used to monitor what is happening to your LOS, servicing systems, CRM systems, and your data. What is being exfiltrated, and by whom? What is being imported, and by whom? What controls exist to monitor and control these processes?

COLLABORATION WITH TRUSTED PARTNERS

Ask your security team if and how information security information is shared within security working groups organized in your industry. MBA has an Information Security Workgroup— The Financial Services Information Sharing and Analysis Center (FS-ISAC).

FS-ISAC describes its function as:

> *The only industry forum for collaboration on critical security threats facing the global financial services sector. When attacks occur, early warning and expert advice can mean the difference between business continuity and widespread business catastrophe. Members of the Financial Services Information Sharing and Analysis Center (FS-ISAC) worldwide receive timely notification and authoritative information specifically designed to help protect critical systems and assets from physical and cyber security threats.*

Leaders in mortgage banking need to ensure that their companies use a secure document management approach. Encrypted email or another secure document system should be used for all customer communication involving PII.

Controlling access to your systems and networks also involves being fully aware of anyone who has access to the systems or networks. This includes vendors. Criminals sometimes attempt to get jobs on cleaning crews for the purpose of breaking into computers for the sensitive information that they expect to find there. Controlling access also includes being careful about having computer or network repair personnel working unsupervised on systems or devices. It is easy for them to steal private/sensitive information.

Companies run by Mavericks usually perform deep pre-employment background and credit checks, including social media searches to identify potentially unfit employee candidates. Require written explanations of any adverse data and consider whether the explanation is credible. Monitor employee compliance carefully during the initial period after hiring to identify potential issues.

Care is to be taken with terminations of employment, both voluntary and involuntary. End of employment should result in termination of access privileges to all company systems, as well as the prompt surrender of organization-owned laptops, phones, and tablets. The email access of terminated employees who owned their own phones and tablets should be terminated immediately.

EASE OF USE VERSUS SECURITY

Mavericks also assess the "ease of use" versus "security" tradeoffs. For example, authentication of users should include multi-factor authentication for important systems. Multifactor authentication creates another step of ID verification, an extra barrier between potential attackers and your data. Encryption is a process of protecting your sensitive business information by using a software program to make the information unreadable to anyone not having the encryption key. With encryption, even if a bad actor somehow obtains your data, it will be unusable without the keys to unencrypt the data. Multi-factor authentication and encryption of data are rapidly becoming must-haves and can be deployed with a reasonable degree of ease of use compared to the elevated security provided.

The Equifax, and many other breaches, were caused by the failure to install patches to known compromises in software and systems. Software and hardware vendors regularly release patches and updates to their supported products to correct security problems and to improve functionality. Once a software patch is released, bad actors review the patch and accompanying information to identify the issue, and armed with this information, they can exploit the vulnerability. This vulnerability will exist inside your organization until you update the appropriate program with the patch. Mavericks ensure that their IT organizations understand how critical it is to apply the patches as soon as possible and employ a corporate standard for deploying patches to all systems in a timely manner. It is critically important that the organization utilizes a trusted third party to verify that organization policies and procedures are actually followed. As Equifax demonstrates, a CEO cannot always rely on IT management to conform to policies and procedures. The CEO must have a competent and reliable third party test the organization's implementation of policy and procedure on a regular basis. Patch management testing is an excellent place to start.

A Bring Your Own Device (BYOD) policy allows employees to use personal devices, such as phones, tablets, computers, etc., to access corporate resources. It is intended to allow employees to use any device they choose to perform their work functions. Lenders need to think carefully about BYOD programs, and if they elect to allow such a program, they need to put in place appropriate policies and procedures to tackle these issues and minimize the risks. Organizations should provide guidance to users on how they can use their own devices to process corporate and personal data. The policy should also be clear to employees that they can only process corporate data for approved corporate purposes.

Another security policy to consider implementing is "least privilege." Least privilege dictates giving each user the least access to data possible while still allowing them to complete their job effectively. By implementing least privilege, an organization better protects the sensitive information of its customers, organization, and partners by limiting the number of people who can access the information and the variety of channels through which data can leave the organization.

In the end, hackers will continue to escalate their attacks. Organizations have to escalate their security efforts. Security is no longer just a cost of doing business. It's an essential element of Strategic Transformation.

THE MAVERICKS

(NOTE: TITLES ARE AS OF INTERVIEW DATE.)

BARRETT BURNS

Mr. Burns serves as the President and Chief Executive Officer of VantageScore Solutions, LLC. Over the years of serving in the industry, he developed extensive experience in banking and finance that allowed him to hold executive positions in a variety of companies. He serves as a board member for numerous industry associations including the Mortgage Bankers Association, the Structured Finance Industry Group Executive Committee, America's Homeowner Alliance, the Corporate Board of Governors for the National Association of Hispanic Real Estate Professionals, and the Asian Real Estate Association of America's National Advisory Council.

BILL COSGROVE

Mr. Cosgrove began his mortgage banking career in 1986 as a residential loan officer. In 1994, he joined Union Home Mortgage Corp. and six years later purchased the company. UHM has grown to 38 states during Bill's leadership. He is a strong industry advocate. He earned the Mortgage Bankers Association's Certified Mortgage Banker certificate. In 2007-2008, Mr. Cosgrove was President of the Ohio Mortgage Bankers Association. In 2008 & 2013, he earned the coveted Hodupp Award for his many contributions to the Ohio MBA. From 2008 to 2010, Bill was the Chairman for MBA's MORPAC Committee and in 2015 Mr. Cosgrove was Chairman of the Mortgage Bankers Association.

BILL EMERSON

Mr. Emerson serves as the Vice Chairman of Rock Holdings Inc., the parent company of Quicken Loans, the nation's second-largest mortgage lender. Bill joined Quicken loans in 1993 and served with passion and commitment to helping customers. His strong leadership skills led Quicken Loans to become the largest retail mortgage lender and has closed nearly $300 Billion in home loan volume across all 50 states since 2013. Bill is a member of the Board of Directors of Xenith, Inc., the Detroit Economic Club, The Parade Company, and the Skillman Foundation.

BRENT CHANDLER

Mr. Chandler has over 20 years of experience in the financial services and technology industries. He is the founder and Chief Executive Officer at FormFree Holdings Corporation, in 2009 he created AccountChek, an investor accepted automated asset verification solution. Mr. Chandler also serves on the advisory board of Jawdrop, an active member of FourAthens Tech Incubator and is an active mentor for Georgia's Terry College of Business Entrepreneurship Program.

CODY PEARCE

Mr. Pearce is the President and Co-founder of Cascade Financial Services, LLC. He is known for his efforts in improving the company's growth and culture. Mr. Pearce currently serves as Chairman of MHI's Financial Services Division, Board member of MHI, is the former Chairman of the MBA's State Legislative and Regulatory Committee, serves on both MORPAC and MHIPac Committees, and is the Former Chairman of the MHI of AZ. Most recently, Mr. Pearce was appointed by the Governor of Arizona to sit on the Arizona Board of Manufactured Housing.

DAVE STEVENS

Mr. Stevens is a former Chief Executive of the Mortgage Bankers Association (MBA) and is currently a mortgage policy consultant. Mr. Stevens served as the Chief Executive Officer and President of the MBA from June 2011 through August 2018. He has a well-rounded background from working with Long & Foster Real Estate, Inc. in the role of Senior Vice President, then as the President and Chief Operating Officer. In addition, he served as the Senior Vice President of Mortgage Sourcing and Single-Family Lending at Freddie Mac. He sits on the Board of Directors for the National Association of Mortgage Brokers (NAMB) and on the lender's advisory council for the Mortgage Bankers Association. He was the Founding Executive Sponsor of the Women's Mortgage Industry

Network and coordinated the first Latino initiative joint venture with Freddie Mac and Latino mortgage industry leaders.

DAVID MOTLEY

Mr. Motley, a Certified Mortgage Banker, has been working with Colonial Savings for more than 15 years. He has been the Executive Vice President and moved his way up to serve as the President of Banking and Mortgage Operations at Colonial Savings, F.A. in May 2006. David Motley has more than 25 years of mortgage production management experience. Motley serves on the board of the Texas Mortgage Bankers Association as the Secretary/Treasurer.

DEB STILL

Ms. Still is the Chief Executive Officer and President of Pulte Mortgage LLC. She has been serving the mortgage industry for more than three four decades. Her background has allowed her to take many roles in Pulte Mortgage LLC. She was an Executive Vice President of Loan Production, Corporate Secretary, and Chief Operating Officer and is a member of the Board of Directors. Ms. Still served as Chairman of the Residential Board of Governors at the Mortgage Bankers Association and was the Chairman of the Mortgage Bankers Association in 2013. She is currently is a member of the MBA's Board of Directors and the Chairman of MBA's Opens Doors Foundation.

ED ROBINSON

Mr. Edward Robinson is the Senior Vice President and Head of Real Estate Lending at USAA. Previously he led Fifth Third Mortgage. Prior to this role, he served as a Senior Vice President of Lending Servicing Operations and as Vice President of Origination. In addition, he has held positions in Genworth Financial and General Electric, where he was responsible for directing operations for the U.S. Mortgage Insurance business, leading strategic initiatives for long-term care insurance, and financial management and analytics.

EDDY PEREZ

Eddy Perez, CMB, is President of Equity Prime Mortgage based in Atlanta, Georgia where he oversees sales, capital markets, diversity and inclusion, marketing, finance and new business. As co-founder of Equity Prime Mortgage, recognized as part of the Inc. 5000, he has excelled within the mortgage industry being named one of the nation's top mortgage bankers, recognized in National Mortgage Professionals Magazine's "40 Most Influential Mortgage Professionals under 40." Throughout his distinguished career he has held multiple executive-level positions. Prior to co-founding Equity Prime Mortgage, in 2008, he operated the top producing affiliate branch for Global Mortgage, Inc. He holds the prestigious Certified Mortgage Banker designation which he earned in October 2014. Perez also holds a seat on the Board of Directors with the MBA.

GENE LUGAT

Mr. Lugat has over thirty years of experience in the mortgage banking industry. He joined PrimeLending, A Plains Capital Company as a Senior Vice President, Regional Production Manager for the Mid-Atlantic Region in 2009. Three years later, he was promoted to the Executive Vice President of the Eastern Division/National Industry and Political Relations with responsibility for production. He served in the National MBA's MORPAC Committee as a board member for the 2015/2016 election cycles and was appointed as Chairman of the National MBA's Mortgage Action Alliance Committee for the 2017/2018 cycles.

JERRY SCHIANO

Mr. Schiano is Chief Executive Officer with over twenty-five years of entrepreneurial experience in the mortgage industry, including founding and leading multiple lending organizations. Mr. Schiano founded (1999) and served as CEO of Wilmington Finance Inc., which grew into a top-15 originator of Non-Agency residential loans. Mr. Schiano sold Wilmington Finance to American General Finance, in 2002 and continued to manage the Company through 2006. Mr. Schiano went on to found New Penn Financial in 2008. New Penn was sold to Shellpoint partners and in the second quarter of this year Shellpoint and New Penn announced that they would be sold to NRZ. Currently, Mr. Schiano is the founder of a new venture focused on direct-to-consumer home equity originations, Spring EQ.

JONATHAN CORR

Mr. Corr serves as the Chief Executive Officer and President of Ellie Mae. Before he became CEO and President, Jonathan served as the Chief Strategy Officer and Executive Vice President of Business Development and Product Strategy for Ellie Mae. He is recognized for his mortgage industry expertise and technology knowledge and has served in management positions for PeopleSoft, Inc., Netscape Communications Corporation and Kana/Broadbase Software/Ruberic.

JULIE PIEPHO

Ms. Piepho is President of National Operations of Cornerstone Home Lending, Inc. She has over 40 years of experience in the Mortgage Banking Industry. In her career, she has led teams of sales and operations to a successful outcome, through her strategic planning and handling of organizational changes. She has received from the MBA both the Andrew D Woodward Distinguished Award and the Schumacher-Bolder Award, in addition to being named a 2018 Women of Influence by HousingWire Magazine. Outside of work, Julie has a passion for volunteering at the Fort Collins Cat Rescue/Spay Neuter Clinic where they pair kittens and Alzheimer's patients together for an afternoon of love and naps!

KEVIN PEARSON

Mr. Pearson served as President of CalAtlantic Mortgage, Inc. (formerly RMC Mortgage and Standard Pacific Mortgage),

CalAtlantic Title (formerly Ryland Title Company and Standard Pacific Title), and CalAtlantic Insurance Services (formerly Ryland Insurance Services), a collective group of legal entities wholly owned by CalAtlantic Group (formerly Standard Pacific, Corp. and The Ryland Group, Inc.). He previously served as an executive in Bank of America's Builder Joint Venture group and as a Senior Vice President of GMAC.

MARTIN KERR

Mr. Kerr is the President of Bestborn Business Solutions, the company behind Loan Vision. Martin has experience in this industry and has a focus in creating efficiencies in the workflow process of the mortgage industry. Before his position at Bestborn, he was a project and business system manager for Technical Plastics.

MATTHEW DURKEE

Mr. Durkee has over 32 years of experience in the Mortgage Banking Industry. He currently serves as the Executive Vice President and President of New England for NBT Bancorp, Inc. He joined the NBT Executive Management Team in 2015 and was promoted to President of New England in 2016. Prior to joining NBT, he was Senior Vice President of regional financial services and President of Chittenden Canada for People's United Bank. He is involved in the United Way of Chittenden County and former Chairman of the Vermont Banker's Association.

NATHAN BURCH

Mr. Burch is currently the Chief Executive Officer and Principal of Vellum Mortgage. Through the efforts of leadership, he has made a positive impact in the positions he's held in his career. Nathan is the founder of McLean Mortgage Corporation, a company that was recognized in 2013 as the "47th Largest Mortgage Lender" by Scotsman Guide and the "10 Best Mortgage Company to Work For" by Mortgage Executive Magazine.

NIMA GHAMSARI

Mr. Ghamsari serves as Chief Executive and Co-founder of Blend, a Silicon Valley Technology company empowering lenders to originate efficiently while keeping a user-friendly interface. Prior to his position at Blend, Nima was a business development engineer and worked as an advisor for the CEO of Palantir Technologies.

PATRICK SINKS

Mr. Sinks has been the Chief Executive Officer and Director of MGIC Investment Corp. He has held many positions within MGIC's finance and accounting organizations, where he was positioned as Senior Vice President, Controller, and Chief Accounting Officer.

PATTY ARVIELO

Patty Arvielo has over 35 years of experience in the mortgage banking industry and is the President & Co-Founder of New American Funding. She is a natural leader with a strong commitment to helping individuals in her industry and community. Throughout her career she has been recognized for her efforts with accolades such as the Prism Award, Elite Woman MPA and Women of Influence. Patty is deeply involved with the National Association of Hispanic Real Estate Professionals. She is on the Diversity and Inclusion Committee and is a former member of the Consumer Affairs Advisory Council for the Mortgage Bankers Association. She serves on the National Park Foundation Board of Directors. She is a former member of the Fannie Mae Affordable Housing Advisory Council and Freddie Mac Community Lender Advisory Board, and currently resides on the Latino Donor Collaborative board.

PHIL DEFRONZO

Mr. DeFronzo is the founder and CEO of Norcom Mortgage. Through natural leadership, Phil was able to grow the company to a well-known regional lender. His achievements include increasing revenue, building brand awareness, and growing the business. In 2011, Norcom was recognized as one of the "Fastest Growing Lenders in New England."

RICK BECHTEL

Rick Bechtel is Executive Vice President, Head of U.S. Mortgage Banking for TD Bank. Prior to TD Bank, he served as Head of

Mortgage Banking at CIBC and The PrivateBank, as well as leadership at Wells Fargo and Chase. He serves on several industry boards and committees and he recently led The PrivateBank to win the inaugural Mortgage Bankers Association Diversity & Inclusion Award. Mr. Bechtel earned his MBA from the Kellogg School of Business at Northwestern University and has expertise in sales, operations, capital markets, compliance, marketing, technology, and product development.

RICK ARVIELO

Rick has over 17 years of experience in the mortgage banking industry, he is an expert in marketing and technology, starting his first company Paradon Industries. Shortly after, Mr. Arvielo joined the mortgage banking industry and launched New American Funding with Patty Arvielo. Rick is a member of the Mortgage Bankers Association (MBA) and is a member of the Board of Directors. In addition, Mr. Arvielo serves in the Mortgage Action Alliance Committee, RESBOG and is the 2017-2018 Chairman of MORPAC, the MBA's Political Action Committee.

ROSE MARIE DAVID

Ms. Rose Marie David has over 30 years of experience in the Mortgage Banking industry. She serves as Senior Executive Vice President of HomeStreet Bank since 2015. She joined HomeStreet Bank in 2012 and shortly after, was then promoted to Senior Vice President and Retail Mortgage Production Leader of HomeStreet bank, then was promoted to the Executive Vice President for Single

Family Lending in 2013. Prior to HomeStreet Bank, she was a Pacific Northwest Regional Sales leader for MetLife Home Loans. She was also an Owner/Executive of Cambridge Mortgage.

ROSS DIEDRICH

Mr. Diedrich is the Chief Executive Officer and co-founder of Covered. Under his leadership, Covered has been recognized on HousingWire's "Tech100" list as one of the most innovative companies in housing, BuiltInColorado's "Top 50" startups to watch in 2018, and has been featured in WIRED Magazine. Previously, Mr. Diedrich was the VP of Structured Products and CD Trading at Nathan Hale Capital where he grew revenue 5.6x and achieved the highest ROI in the company. He regularly ranked as one of the top 3 traders in the country. During his tenure at Nathan Hale Capital, he achieved the prestigious Chartered Financial Analyst designation.

STANLEY MIDDLEMAN

Stanley C. Middleman is the founder and Chief Executive Officer of Freedom Mortgage Corporation, a national, full-service mortgage company headquartered in Mount Laurel, NJ. The company is one of the largest mortgage originators and mortgage servicers in the US. Mr. Middleman has over 30 years' experience in the financial services industry. Stan is a member of the Housing Policy Executive Council and serves on the NAHREP Corporate Board of Governors. He has served on numerous advisory boards, including Freddie Mac and Ellie Mae Inc. In November 2018, Freedom Mortgage will be presented with the

Chairman's Award in honor of their service to our community and their support of Liberty USO. Mr. Middleman is a graduate of Temple University with a BS in Accounting.

STEVE SCHWALB

Mr. Schwalb has more than 20 years of experience in residential lending. He co-founded Angel Oak Home Loans in 2011 and is the CEO and Managing partner. He also co-founded Angel Oak Mortgage Solutions, a non-agency wholesale and correspondent mortgage lender, and Angel Oak Prime Bridge, a commercial residential lender providing financing solutions for real estate investors. In 2015, Angel Oak originated over $1 billion in mortgages across the lending companies. He played an integral role in Angel Oak's first securitization of non-prime whole loans, which was a collaborative effort between sister companies Angel Oak Mortgage Solutions, Angel Oak Capital Advisors, LLC and Angel Oak Home Loans. The approximate $150 million securitization of Angel Oak originated loans was one of the largest mortgage securitizations since the 2008 financial crisis.

SUSAN STEWART

Ms. Stewart is the CEO of SWBC Mortgage Corporation. Susan has impacted her company tremendously. She is well known for her commitment amongst her customers and co-workers. She serves as Vice Chair of the Residential Board of Governors of the MBA and is an MBA Board Member and is an Opens Door Foundation Board Member. Ms. Stewart is a past president of the Texas Mortgage Bankers Association and the San Antonio Mortgage Bankers.

TIM NGUYEN

Mr. Nguyen is the CEO & Co-Founder of BeSmartee, a leader in digital mortgage innovation. Using a combination of big data and AI, borrowers can go from application, to approval to disclosures, and enter fulfillment in about 15 minutes. Previously, he was CEO & Co-Founder of InHouse, Inc., a technology-enabled, service company providing appraisal management solutions to the mortgage lending industry. He has served as an advisor to companies ranging from $5 to $500 million in annual revenue. He lives in Southern California with his wife and two boys.

APPENDIX 2
THE FINANCIAL CRISIS OF 2007-2010 AND BEYOND

The extreme stress in the financial markets in the late summer and early fall of 2008 was quantified by the Kansas City Financial Stress Index (KCFSI), a monthly measure of stress in the U.S. financial system based on 11 financial market variables issued by the Kansas City Federal Reserve Bank. A positive value indicates that financial stress is above the long-run average, while a negative value signifies that financial stress is below the long-run average. The KCFSI decreased from 1.47 in April 2008 to 0.94 in May 31, 2008, followed by an almost six-fold increase to an all-time high of 5.55 as of October 2008. This unexpected and unprecedented increase in financial stress as quantified by the KCFSI was the proximate cause of rapid declines in asset prices.

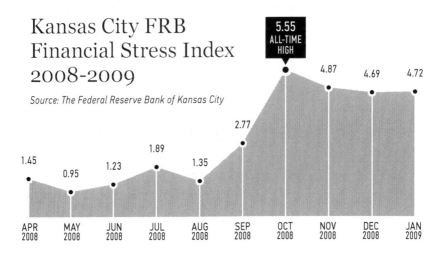

Kansas City FRB
Financial Stress Index
2008-2009

5.55
ALL-TIME
HIGH

Source: The Federal Reserve Bank of Kansas City

1.45
0.95
1.23
1.89
1.35
2.77
4.87
4.69
4.72

APR
2008
MAY
2008
JUN
2008
JUL
2008
AUG
2008
SEP
2008
OCT
2008
NOV
2008
DEC
2008
JAN
2009

The failure of several subprime mortgage lenders in 2007 reduced the availability of credit to subprime borrowers. New Century Financial Corporation, a real estate investment trust founded in 1995 and headquartered in Irvine, California, declared bankruptcy on April 2, 2007. On July 11, 2007, credit rating agencies S&P and Moody's announced the downgrade of $12 billion and $5 billion of subprime RMBS, respectively. Bear Stearns placed two structured and asset-backed securities hedge funds in bankruptcy on July 31, 2007. American Home Mortgage Investment Corp., a large subprime lender, filed for bankruptcy on August 6, 2007. In 2007, losses on subprime mortgage-related financial assets began to cause strains in the global financial markets. In December 2007, the U.S. economy entered a recession.

Despite the failures cited above, the markets in early 2008 did not act as if the economy was in severe trouble. On January 11, 2008, for example, Bank of America announced an agreement to purchase Countrywide Financial Corp for $4 billion in stock. Bear Stearns was acquired by JPMorgan Chase on March 16, 2008. The Federal

Reserve agreed to guarantee $30 billion of Bear Stearns' assets in connection with the government-sponsored sale of the investment bank to JPMorgan Chase.

As of late May 2008, the financial markets continued to show signs of stress, but the stress was largely confined to the subprime market, and significant actions by the Federal Reserve and other central banks appeared to be addressing subprime mortgage matters. For example, the Federal Reserve responded to an apparent lack of liquidity in worldwide financial markets with sharp reductions in the federal funds rate, reducing the rate from 5.25% in May 2007 to 2.00% as of April 30, 2008. The Federal Reserve press release stated, "The substantial easing of monetary policy to date, combined with ongoing measures to foster market liquidity, should help to promote moderate growth over time and to mitigate risks to economic activity." On May 8, 2008, the Federal Reserve provided an increase in the amounts auctioned to eligible depository institutions under its biweekly Term Auction Facility (TAF) to bring the amounts outstanding under the TAF to $150 billion, again to increase liquidity.

For example, prior to the failure of Fannie Mae, the company issued the following unexpected and extraordinary description of events occurring after the close of its second quarter 2008 (the note below was included in Fannie Mae's June 30, 2008, Form 10-Q, released August 9, 2008):

Market Events of July 2008:

> *In mid-July, following the close of the second quarter, liquidity and trading levels in the capital markets became extremely volatile, and the functioning of the markets was disrupted. The market value of our common stock dropped*

rapidly, to its lowest level since October 1990, and we experienced reduced demand for our unsecured debt and MBS products. This market disruption caused a significant increase in our cost of funding and a substantial increase in mark-to-market losses on our trading securities arising from a significant widening of credit spreads. In addition, during July, credit performance continued to deteriorate, and we recorded charge-offs and foreclosed property expenses that were higher than we had experienced in any month during the second quarter and higher than we expected, driven by higher defaults and higher loan loss severities in markets most affected by the steep home price declines. Greater credit losses in July not only reduce our July net income through our actual realized losses, but also affect us as we expect that we will need to make further increases to our combined loss reserves in the second half of 2008 to incorporate our experience in July.

Less than 30 days after this 10-Q release, in early September 2008, Fannie Mae was in unexpected conservatorship. In addition, four other major publicly traded companies were unexpectedly placed in conservatorship, bankruptcy, or were acquired under duress. The companies and their impact on the financial services marketplace listed below in September 2008 were extraordinary:

- Freddie Mac and Fannie Mae owned or guaranteed $4 trillion in mortgage loans at the time of their failure, or 40% of all residential mortgage loans outstanding in the U.S.

- AIG had assets of over $1 trillion at the time of its takeover.

- Washington Mutual and Wachovia assets totaled over $1 trillion at the time of their takeover.

The failure of these five financial firms, with a collective total of $6 trillion of assets heavily involved in the U.S. housing market, in one month, September 6 to October 7, 2008, had an overwhelming adverse impact on liquidity and price discovery in financial markets.

The unexpected nature of the stress in the financial markets is illustrated in the sharp climb in bank failures. Total assets of failed banks from the beginning of 2007 through June 1, 2008 were just under $5 billion. By October 1, 2008, the total assets of failed banks had grown to $350 billion, an increase of 70 times. A total of 7 banks failed from January 1, 2005 to June 4, 2008. Another 27 failed from June 1, 2008 to January 31, 2009. Ultimately, 468 banks with total assets of $690 billion failed from January 1, 2005 through December 31, 2012.

On July 11, 2008, IndyMac Bank, F.S.B., Pasadena, CA, was closed by the Office of Thrift Supervision. The Federal Deposit Insurance Corporation was named conservator. IndyMac Bank, FSB had total assets of $32.01 billion and total deposits of $19.06 billion as of March 31, 2008. The prior FDIC-insured failure in California was the Southern Pacific Bank, Torrance, on February 7, 2003.

On July 13, 2008, the Board of Governors of the Federal Reserve System announced that it had granted the Federal Reserve Bank of New York the authority to lend to Fannie Mae and Freddie Mac should such lending prove necessary and that any lending would be at the primary credit rate and collateralized by U.S. government and federal agency securities. This authorization was intended to supplement the Treasury's existing lending authority and to help ensure the ability of Fannie Mae and Freddie Mac to promote the availability of home mortgage credit during a period of stress in financial markets. At the same time, the U.S. Treasury Department announced a temporary increase in the credit lines of Fannie Mae and Freddie Mac and a temporary authorization for the Treasury to purchase equity in either GSE if needed.

On July 15, 2008, the Securities and Exchange Commission issued an emergency order to enhance investor protections against "naked" short selling in the securities of Fannie Mae, Freddie Mac, and primary dealers at commercial and investment banks.

On July 30, 2008, President Bush signed the Housing and Economic Recovery Act of 2008, Public Law 110-289, which, among other provisions, authorized the Treasury to purchase GSE obligations and reformed the regulatory supervision of the GSEs under a new Federal Housing Finance Agency.

On July 30, 2008, the Federal Reserve announced several steps to enhance the effectiveness of its existing liquidity facilities, including the introduction of longer terms to maturity in its Term Auction Facility Extension of the Primary Dealer Credit Facility (PDCF) and the Term Securities Lending Facility (TSLF).

The Federal Housing Finance Agency (FHFA) initiated the conservatorships of the Federal National Mortgage Association (Fannie Mae) and the Federal Home Loan Mortgage Corporation (Freddie Mac) on September 6, 2008. The U.S. Treasury Department announced three additional measures to complement the FHFA's decision: 1) preferred stock purchase agreements between the Treasury/FHFA and Fannie Mae and Freddie Mac to ensure the GSEs positive net worth; 2) a new secured lending facility available to Fannie Mae, Freddie Mac, and the Federal Home Loan Banks; and 3) a temporary program to purchase GSE MBS.

On September 14, 2008, the Federal Reserve Board announced a significant broadening in the collateral accepted under its existing liquidity program for primary dealers and financial markets to provide additional support to financial markets.

On September 15, 2008, Bank of America announced its intent to purchase Merrill Lynch & Co. for $50 billion.

Also, on September 15, 2008, Lehman Brothers filed for federal bankruptcy protection.

Credit rating agencies downgraded AIG's long-term credit rating on the afternoon of September 15, 2008. AIG's stock price plunged. AIG could not access short-term liquid funds in the credit markets.

On September 16, 2008, the Federal Reserve Board, with the full support of the Treasury Department, authorized the Federal Reserve Bank of New York to lend up to $85 billion to AIG under section 13(3) of the Federal Reserve Act.

The net asset value of shares in the Reserve Primary Money Fund fell below $1, primarily due to losses on Lehman Brothers commercial paper and medium-term notes, further disrupting liquidity in the money markets.

On September 17, 2008, the Securities and Exchange Commission took several coordinated actions to strengthen investor protections against "naked" short selling. The Commission's actions applied to the securities of all public companies, including all companies in the financial sector. The actions were effective at 12:01 a.m. ET on Thursday, September 18, 2008.

On September 18, 2008, the Bank of Canada, the Bank of England, the European Central Bank (ECB), the Federal Reserve, the Bank of Japan, and the Swiss National Bank announced coordinated measures designed to address the continued elevated pressures in U.S. dollar short-term funding markets and to improve the liquidity conditions in global financial markets.

On September 19, 2008, the Federal Reserve Board announced two enhancements to its programs to provide liquidity to markets. One initiative extended non-recourse loans at the primary credit rate to U.S. depository institutions and bank holding companies to finance their purchases of high-quality asset-backed commercial paper (ABCP) from money market mutual funds. To further support market functioning, the Federal Reserve agreed to purchase from primary dealers' quantities of federal agency discount notes, which are short-term debt obligations issued by Fannie Mae, Freddie Mac, and the Federal Home Loan Banks.

On September 19, 2008, the U.S. Treasury Department established a temporary guarantee program for the U.S. money market mutual fund industry. Concerns about the net asset value of money market funds falling below $1 exacerbated global financial market turmoil and caused severe liquidity strains in world markets. In turn, these pressures caused a spike in some short-term interest and funding rates and significantly heightened volatility in exchange markets. Maintenance of the standard $1 net asset value for money market mutual funds was important to investors. If the net asset value for a fund fell below $1, this undermined investor confidence. The program provided support to investors in funds that participated in the program and those funds would not "break the buck." This action was to enhance market confidence and alleviate investors' concerns about the ability for money market mutual funds to absorb a loss.

The Exchange Stabilization Fund was established by the Gold Reserve Act of 1934. This Act authorizes the Secretary of the Treasury, with the approval of the President, "to deal in gold, foreign exchange, and other instruments of credit and securities" consistent with the obligations of the U.S. government in the International Monetary Fund to promote international financial stability.

On September 20, 2008, the Treasury Department submitted legislation to Congress requesting the authority to purchase troubled assets from financial institutions to promote market stability and help protect American families and the US economy.

On September 25, 2008, JPMorgan Chase acquired the banking operations of Washington Mutual Bank in a transaction facilitated by the Federal Deposit Insurance Corporation. JPMorgan Chase acquired the assets, assumed the qualified financial contracts, and made a payment of $1.9 billion. Claims by equity and subordinated and senior debt holders were not acquired. Washington Mutual Bank also had a subsidiary; Washington Mutual FSB, Park City, Utah. They had combined assets of $307 billion and total deposits of $188 billion.

On September 29, 2008, central banks announced further coordinated actions to expand significantly the capacity to provide U.S. dollar liquidity. The Federal Reserve announced several initiatives to support financial stability and to maintain a stable flow of credit to the economy during this period of significant strain in global markets. Actions by the Federal Reserve included: (1) an increase in the size of the 84-day maturity TAF auctions to $75 billion per auction from $25 billion beginning with the October 6 auction, (2) two forward TAF auctions totaling $150 billion to be conducted in November to provide term funding over year-end, and (3) an increase in swap authorization limits with the Bank of Canada, Bank of England, Bank of Japan, Danmarks Nationalbank (National Bank of Denmark), European Central Bank (ECB), Norges Bank (Bank of Norway), Reserve Bank of Australia, Sveriges Riksbank (Bank of

Sweden), and Swiss National Bank to a total of $620 billion, from $290 billion previously.

On September 29, 2008, Citigroup Inc. announced its intent to acquire the banking operations of Wachovia Corporation; Charlotte, North Carolina, in a transaction facilitated by the Federal Deposit Insurance Corporation and concurred with by the Board of Governors of the Federal Reserve and the Secretary of the Treasury in consultation with the President. Wells Fargo & Company offered a competing bid on October 3, 2008, which ultimately was accepted.

The Troubled Asset Relief Program (TARP) was signed into law by U.S. President George W. Bush on October 3, 2008. TARP provided up to $700 billion to inject equity into the U.S. banks and to purchase 'troubled assets.'

On October 3, 2008, President George W. Bush signed the Emergency Economic Stabilization Act of 2008, which temporarily raised the basic limit on federal deposit insurance coverage from $100,000 to $250,000 per depositor. The temporary increase in deposit insurance coverage became effective upon the President's signature. The legislation provided that the basic deposit insurance limit would return to $100,000 after December 31, 2009. In fact, the 'temporary' limit has remained at $250,000.

On October 7, 2008, the Federal Reserve Board announced the creation of the Commercial Paper Funding Facility (CPFF), a facility that would complement the Federal Reserve's existing credit facilities to help provide liquidity to term funding markets.

On October 14, 2008, the Treasury announced a voluntary Capital Purchase Program to encourage U.S. financial institutions to build capital to increase the flow of financing to U.S. businesses and consumers and to support the U.S. economy. Under the program, Treasury purchased up to $250 billion of senior preferred shares on standardized terms as described in the program's term sheet. The senior preferred shares would qualify as Tier 1 capital.

On October 24, 2008, PNC Financial Services Group Inc. purchased National City Corporation, creating the fifth largest U.S. bank.

On November 10, 2008, the Federal Reserve Board and the U.S. Treasury Department announced a restructuring of the government's financial support of AIG. The Treasury was to purchase $40 billion of AIG preferred shares under the TARP program, a portion of which was to be used to reduce the Federal Reserve's loan to AIG from $85 billion to $60 billion. The Federal Reserve Board also authorized the Federal Reserve Bank of New York to establish two new lending facilities for AIG: The Residential Mortgage-Backed Securities Facility was to lend up to $22.5 billion to a newly formed limited liability company to purchase residential MBS from AIG; the Collateralized Debt Obligations Facility was to lend up to $30 billion to a newly formed LLC to purchase CDOs from AIG, Maiden Lane III LLC.

On November 18, 2008, Executives of Ford, General Motors, and Chrysler testified before Congress requesting access to the TARP for federal loans.

On November 20, 2008, Fannie Mae and Freddie Mac announced that they would suspend mortgage foreclosures until January 2009.

On November 21, 2008, the U.S. Treasury Department announced that it would help liquidate The Reserve Fund's 'U.S. Government Fund'. The Treasury served as a buyer of last resort for the fund's securities to ensure the orderly liquidation of the fund.

On November 21, 2008, the U.S. Treasury Department, Federal Reserve Board, and FDIC jointly announced an agreement with Citigroup that provided a package of guarantees, liquidity access, and capital. Citigroup issued preferred shares to the Treasury and FDIC in exchange for protection against losses on a $306 billion pool of commercial and residential securities held by Citigroup. The Federal Reserve was to backstop residual risk in the asset pool through a non-recourse loan. In addition, the Treasury committed up to an additional $20 billion in Citigroup from the TARP.

On November 25, 2008, the Federal Reserve Board announced the creation of the Term Asset-Backed Securities Lending Facility (TALF), under which the Federal Reserve Bank of New York would lend up to $200 billion on a non-recourse basis to holders of AAA-rated asset-backed securities and recently originated consumer and small business loans. The U.S. Treasury would provide $20 billion of TARP money for credit protection.

On November 25, 2008, the Federal Reserve Board announced a new program to purchase direct obligations of housing-related government-sponsored enterprises —Fannie Mae, Freddie Mac, and Federal Home Loan Banks—and MBS backed by the GSEs. Purchases of up to $100 billion in GSE direct obligations were to be conducted as auctions among Federal Reserve primary dealers. Purchases of up to $500 billion in MBS were to be conducted by asset managers.

On December 3, 2008, the SEC approved measures to increase transparency and accountability at credit rating agencies to ensure that firms provided more meaningful ratings and greater disclosure to investors.

On December 19, 2008, the U.S. Treasury Department authorized loans of up to $13.4 billion for General Motors and $4.0 billion for Chrysler from the TARP.

On December 29, 2008, the U.S. Treasury Department announced that it would purchase $5 billion in equity from GMAC as part of its program to assist the domestic automotive industry. The Treasury also agreed to lend up to $1 billion to General Motors "so that GM can participate in a rights offering at GMAC in support of GMAC's reorganization as a bank holding company." This commitment was in addition to the support announced on December 19, 2008.

By any view, it was a hell of a six-month period.

I am impressed and excited by the Maverick CEOs This is my second book that included their experiences and insights. They are awesome.

Two truths came to me after I wrote this book.

The first was that the talent to transform our industry exists. The Maverick CEO's prove that.

The second was that we need to marshal that talent and turn it into action. Fast. We have a 'need for speed' in our industry.

These truths led me to create a new website, MaverickCEO.com.

I invite you to take a look at the website. Our mission is to make it a resource for us all as we transform our industry.

Jim Deitch

P.S. If you have any ideas that you want to share about how you 'manage differently' please send me an email at jim.deitch@maverickceo.com

Learn more about the Mavericks and stay connected with the latest ideas that will transform the mortgage banking industry. The website features biographies of all the Mavericks, some of their thought leadership ideas and The 'Thinking Differently' blog.

MaverickCEO.com

PRAISE FOR
DIGITALLY TRANSFORMING
THE MORTGAGE BANKING INDUSTRY:
The Maverick's Quest for Outstanding Profit and Customer Satisfaction

"Informative, well researched and entertaining...with a clear road-map for increased profit and customer satisfaction excellence..."
— Bill Emerson,
Vice Chairman of Quicken Loans Inc.

" The book uses powerful examples from the industry thought leaders on transforming the mortgage banking business to a high profit, high customer satisfaction model."
— Kevin Pearson,
President of CalAtlantic Mortgage

"Jim Deitch takes readers through the challenges that customers and lenders are facing in the Mortgage Banking Industry"
— Patrick Sinks,
CEO of MGIC Investment Corporation

" A comprehensive survey of industry thought leaders presented in a clear and concise manner."
— Steve Shank,
President & CEO of Flinchbaugh Engineering, Inc.

"Jim Deitch takes you inside the back offices, strategy and industry leaders prospective of the top mortgage banking firms in America. A must read for the industry and consumers."
— Bill Cosgrove,
President & CEO of Union Home Mortgage Corp.

"The book provides in-depth knowledge from industry thought leaders. It balances technology and process very appropriately."
— Tim Nguyen,
CEO & Co Founder BeSmartee

"Simple yet informative, and conceptual yet practical, Transforming the Mortgage Banking Industry is a book designed to help a lender achieve best in class profits and customer satisfaction"
— Phil DeFronzo,
Normcom Mortgage

"Navigating the landscape of digital transformation is incredibly complex. Jim was able to synthesize thought leaders from all angles into one guide."
-Nima Ghamsari, CEO of Blend

"Detailed, Powerful, and Concise. Read it and share it with your executives. Jim describes the future landscape of lending, and how to prosper in the coming Digital Mortgage revolution."
— Nathan Burch,
CEO of Vellum Mortgage LLC

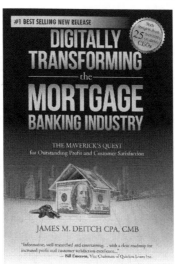

PRE-PUBLICATION REVIEWS OF STRATEGICALLY TRANSFORMING THE MORTGAGE BANKING INDUSTRY:
Thought Leadership on Disruption from Maverick CEOs

"Jim has captured how strategy and disruption will be game changers in the industry. This is a must read"

Brent Chandler,
CEO & Founder
FormFree Holding Corporation

"Excellent context, especially the continued focus on disruption and how it happens. Good read, good data. Every lending exec should read it."

Dave Stevens,
President and Chief Executive Officer, (retired)
Mortgage Bankers Association

"A must read. Must be shared. The shape of things to come for innovative mortgage lenders."

Julie Piepho,
President of National Operations
Cornerstone Home Lending, Inc.

"Jim has synthesized the thoughts of 30 leaders into a great guide for the key strategic levers of mortgage industry success."

Marcia Davies,
Chief Operating Officer
Mortgage Bankers Association

"The book takes readers through the challenges, routes and rewards of the strategic transformation."

Patty Arvielo,
President and Co-Founder
New American Funding

"This book is an eye opener for executives in a turbulent industry."

Rick Arvielo,
CEO
New American Funding

"This book is a must-read for those who seek to optimize strategy within the collision of fintech tools and next-level data analytics."

Richard Bechtel
EVP
Head of US Mortgage Banking
TD Bank

Made in the USA
Columbia, SC
11 December 2018